HAPPY PEOPLE WORK HARDER

THE LEADER'S GUIDE TO INSPIRING POSITIVE CHANGE

GAREN JEMIAN

ISBN 978-1-9995161-0-9
I. Business / II. Self-Help
Printed in Canada and USA.

Design by Señor Garbanzo El Toro.

ACKNOWLEDGEMENTS

To my wife Marisa, thank you for your unshakeable support and encouragement throughout my journey. This book could not have been made possible without you.

To my family and friends, thank you for surrounding me with love and support. You fill my life with joy, and I'm forever grateful.

To my teachers and mentors, thank you for playing your part in my accumulation of knowledge. May this book serve as an echo of your wisdom.

To my clients, thank you for allowing me to learn and grow from our interactions. These pages would be empty without the work we've done together.

And finally, to you, the reader. Thank you for unknowingly motivating me to assemble these pages.

CONTENTS

INTRODUCTION

The only way to do great work is to love what you do.
~ Steve Jobs ~

Can you think of a time when you were at your best, and you were downright miserable? Have you ever heard someone say: "I became successful by doing something I don't care for and put very little love into"? If Steve Jobs didn't find joy in his work, he would have never reshaped the world with his creations. If Lebron James didn't love basketball and find pleasure in it, he would have never become one of the best players of his generation. And if you're not deeply satisfied and engaged in what you do, you are not only wasting your time, but you are denying the world of your incredible abilities and potential.

Happy people work harder. They do so because their work energizes and inspires them. They tend to be more creative, productive and committed to their objectives. More accountable for their results. They tend to take less sick days and ultimately stay on-board longer. Equipping leaders with the capacity to tap into their employees' strengths, passions, and values, and maximizing their potential is imperative to achieving these positive outcomes.

It starts with a deeper understanding of human motivation, positive relationships, effective communication, and some basic coaching. It's about seeing beyond the traditional metrics of success and embracing the world of intangibles, such as emotional wellness and fulfillment. It's about identifying and contributing to the key drivers that fuel the core components in a well-oiled, highly efficient, energized and inspired team.

A GROWING NEED

Corporate culture is in a state of transition leaving many organizations in the dark with regards to modern methods of management, leadership, and motivation. This growing trend is underlined by the common struggle to adapt to the culture and mindset of future generations. The results are high turnover rates and absenteeism along with reduced engagement, productivity, performance and job satisfaction.

An onslaught of research is emerging with staggering facts about our current crisis. Gallup, a leading organization in employee behaviour found that 87% of employees worldwide are not engaged at work. That means that 87% of the workforce is either paddling in the opposite direction or not paddling at all. Michelle McQuaid, the author of Five Reasons to Tell Your Boss To Go F**k Themselves found that 65% of employees would rather see their boss replaced than receive a pay raise. Additionally, 60% said they would do a better job if they got along better with their boss.

Shocked by these findings, I decided to put these statistics to the test. I reached out to an old friend who operates his recruitment firm and asked if I could work with him to conduct a study. He kindly agreed. Just like that, I was a recruitment consultant. One of my roles was to contact potential candidates and offer them new career opportunities. A good portion of my target clientele already had jobs which put me in a perfect position to get a pulse on the matter. What I found was mind-boggling. On average, one out of two people I contacted were ready and willing to leave their jobs. When I asked "why?", over 70% of them said that they would jump ship because of a negative relationship with their leaders. Their comments were droningly repetitive and downright painful to hear. The gist of the feedback I gathered is as follows:

My boss:

- Doesn't appreciate me.
- Lacks communication skills.
- Doesn't challenge me.
- Isn't understanding.
- Doesn't mentor me.
- Lacks respect and professionalism.
- Doesn't care about my opinions.
- Doesn't tap into my strengths.

While poor leadership didn't account for all the reasons for quitting, it had a significant role to play in it. The biggest surprise was that very few ever mentioned money. Many were even willing to take a slight pay cut in exchange for more favourable conditions. The conclusion is clear that inevitable change is upon us and that a new approach must be adopted if businesses and their leaders are going to thrive in the 21st century. Beyond recruitment, there is a dire need for leadership development to promote employee fulfillment and retention.

A BRIEF HISTORY OF MOTIVATION

Since the dawn of civilization, humankind has primarily used two methods of motivation: threats and bribes, or if you prefer, fear and money. Both are so incredibly effective because they leverage a person's need for survival and comfort. From the Egyptian Empire to our current technological revolution, the tried, tested and true methods still reign to this day. They're still here because they work. Fear and money are two of the most powerful forces when it comes to getting people to do what we want them to and as long as we live in a society where the mighty dollar rules, money shall remain a dominant motivator.

An extreme example of fear motivation is an armed robber mugging you for your wallet. You need to survive. He needs your money. A match made in heaven. Instant motivation. Instant results. Violence and physical dominance is a heck of a way to get things done. With regards to everyday life, can we honestly say that fear doesn't exist in the workplace? That employees don't feel some form of threat on a daily basis? "Do your job or else..." is either heard or felt and as long as the employee lacks a sense of security, it works like a charm.

As for bribes, well, that one is indeed all around us. What is a job after all? It's where you trade in hours of your life for money. We then use this money to pay for things that allow us to sustain a certain level of comfort and perhaps some luxury. The system is dependant on our yearning for this comfort. Now it's not the company's fault the entire world works on this system. It works, and it's way better than global slavery. However, offering money to have someone do something they don't honestly want to do is essentially the definition of a bribe.

THE SILENT REVOLUTION

Times are quickly changing. We now live in an era when most everything is a quick fix and increasingly disposable, and that includes employment. Job offers are emailed to us daily. Meetings are increasingly facilitated by video-conferencing, and our productivity is ever-enhanced by software. Education is now accessible to all who have wifi and a device. Communication, education, productivity, and entertainment, among other things, are cheaper and easier to access than ever before.

More than ever, people are empowered with connectivity, choice, and comfort. Whether we want to place blame on the technological revolution or not, we can't argue with the fact that we live in a time when loyalty through security is slowly dropping on people's priority lists, or at least, a time when other values are emerging. Values that were once overlooked for the sake of financial security and survival are now coming out of the shadows, and it's precisely why your employees don't respond to these traditional tactics. And unless we experience a severe global economic crisis, one that would bring about a time of desperation and duty, this trend will remain a constant.

We are currently experiencing a silent revolution of the workforce. One that is driven by the fulfillment and empowerment of the employee, and if harnessed correctly, can be used to propel your organization to new heights. Resistance to this trend will only push your greatest assets to your nearest competitor who is willing to embrace a new, more desirable corporate culture. Top-down management is becoming obsolete within organizations who can foresee and embrace the future and sadly, those who fail to adapt will be left with an aging workforce that won't soon be replaced. The billion dollar question "how do I motivate someone?" is being rephrased as "how do I motivate someone when money and fear are slowly losing their power?"

Every single one of us has tremendous potential. We all have the ability to inspire positive change in the world around us. And we can all benefit by having someone who can help us do just that. Someone to help create awareness and perspective. Someone who can help us tap into our deepest desires and motives. One who challenges us to reach beyond our limitations, to hold us accountable and encourage us to claim ownership over our successes. Someone who can inspire us to become the most authentic version of ourselves. And your team needs you to be that person.

I wrote this book for those who are looking for ways to improve life at work, either for themselves or others. As a tool for self-awareness, for leaders and employees alike. To those of you who have the power to conduct one-on-ones with team members, may this book serve as a doorway to maximizing your potential as well as theirs. This book carries with it the hope of inspiring positive change and humanizing the corporate experience for current and future generations. My intention is one of creating awareness and tapping into your highest potential as a leader, as a peer, as a human being in search of a better way.

CHAPTER ONE

THE EVOLUTION OF MOTIVATION

WHY WE DO THE THINGS WE DO

There is no way to happiness. Happiness is the way.

~ Thich Nhat Hanh ~

Why do we do the things we do? A question to which the answer would solve many of the woes in our professional lives. A question that is at the root of another, more common one: "how do I motivate someone?" When leaders ask me this, and sooner or later they surely do, I answer their question with one of my own: "why does anyone do anything?" For us to learn how to motivate others, we must first understand what motivation is and how it works. In it's purest form, it's our willingness to do something. Our justification. Our *why*.

Why do you do it?

Because _______ .

Why do I arrive fifteen minutes earlier than I have to before a meeting? I don't want to be late. I want to take my time and not worry about traffic. I like to get there early to mentally prepare myself for my client. I want to be professional and punctual. All great reasons but there's something under all of those layers. Why do I really do it? The word *really* can't be stressed enough. It's the heart of the matter, and it's the key that unlocks every door behind motivation. There could be an infinite array of reasons behind human behaviour. So how can we harness motivation without a mastery of psychology? If you've ever been a part of a psychometric test in your office, you have a pretty good idea of the complex algorithms that have been assembled by teams of professionals. The results are often so daunting that to put them into practical use, you'd need to study the material for months before truly harnessing it. I'm here to tell you that there is a more natural solution. And it requires nothing more than grasping a simple concept that applies to absolutely everyone walking this earth.

THE LAW OF MOTIVATION

Imagine for a moment that there was a common denominator. A universal motive behind all of our decisions and actions. One that could serve as a guiding light for all those who want to better understand themselves and the world around them. One that could help leaders tap into the highest potential of their people. One that could serve as a catalyst to becoming your greatest self. Just like gravity, there exists such a law, and it states:

> Every decision and action is driven by the desire
> to maximize pleasure and to minimize pain.

We naturally and instinctively move towards pleasure and away from pain. You don't need to dig deeper than your reality to figure this one out. Is it not common knowledge that we follow this pattern? Wouldn't you rather live than die? Be comfortably warm than freezing outdoors? Well fed rather than starving? Wouldn't you rather have an inspirational leader than an order-barking boss? Wouldn't you prefer to love what you do than wake up every morning dreading your life?

Why do you do it?

Because it makes me happy.

Joy. Happiness. Pleasure. These words are used freely and interchangeably in this book. They are merely meant to point in the direction of desirability. One of positive emotional impact. If these words don't resonate with you, perhaps think of the word *positivity,* or better yet, *relative positivity*. It is highly personal and entirely based on our perceptions and definitions.

Beneath all our actions, relative joy is the reason we want anything. The zebra runs away from the hungry lion to survive. The single parent works two jobs to provide comfort and support for their child. The miserable employee keeps plowing away at their daily grind to maintain a steady income. The terminally ill patient chooses euthanasia to stop the suffering. All examples of the deeper motive that connects all of our decisions and actions.

Here's a fun fact: If I were to ask you the question "why?" enough times about whatever it is that you're doing, your answer would always end up sounding like "...because it makes me happy" or a derivative of it. It's not about bliss. It's not about being ecstatic. It's about relativity. It's about our levels of satisfaction based on our perceptions and personal standards. We're in search for the best case scenario at all times; of the most desirable outcome for our circumstances.

Our minds continuously assess and predict whether a course of action will increase, maintain or decrease our relative levels of joy. Our brains are machines built for comparing possible outcomes which help us figure out which decisions and actions to take. We are in the constant pursuit of happiness where all of the options presented to us are subjected to this comparison. If we believe a given action will increase our levels of joy or at least minimize our pain, then we are more likely to choose to do so. If we believe a given action will decrease our levels of joy or increase our suffering, then we are less likely to choose that path. Our gravitation towards pleasure explains why we do the things we do. The choices we make and the actions we take.

THERE IS ONLY ONE "WHY"

There is only one ultimate reason we want to have, do or be anything. It's the same reason you live where you do. It's the reason why you're in a relationship with your significant other. It's the reason why your hair is shaped that way, why you drive that car, why you eat certain foods and why you may have skipped the gym this morning. It's a force of nature no different from gravity. From basic needs like survival, food, clothing, and shelter to comfort and luxury, the pursuit of happiness and the avoidance of pain have dictated every single decision and action since the dawn of life. Evolution relies on it. No matter who you are or what you do, relative joy is the driver behind the wheel.

I urge you to pause here. Take a moment and try to break this pattern. Think of any one of your decisions or ask someone around you why they do what they do. Ask about the reasoning behind it and how it adds value to their lives. Ask them "why?". Pick anything from why there's mustard on their hot dog to why they choose to continue smoking even though they know it might kill them. Whatever answer they give you, keep asking until there is no higher motive. Where gravitation towards pleasure and away from pain becomes apparent and when they finally spew out the inevitable response: "because it makes me happy."

As a leader, this truth is a gateway to understanding motivation at the office and beyond. Accepting and embracing it allows us to approach our professional lives with a new lens. One that humanizes the experience and provides a possibility of a happier workplace. Start noticing the world around you. Observe with heightened awareness, that everything happening around you is driven by one powerful force of nature. Take comfort in the knowledge that if there's one thing that unites all living entities, it's that we all strive for the maximum amount of pleasure and least amount of pain at any given moment and throughout our lifetimes.

CONVENTIONAL METHODS

Our constant pursuit of happiness explains why we do the things we do. How can we leverage this knowledge in the workplace? As leaders, we place a tremendous amount of responsibility on our shoulders to motivate those around us. Not only do we have to meet the demands of our superiors and our clients, but have the added pleasure of trying to get everyone engaged, autonomous and productive. That's quite possibly the reason why you're reading this book. We're searching for answers to the question everyone is asking:

> How do I motivate someone?

This question is the starting point of our quest for converting disengaged people into highly motivated ones. While motivation is defined as the willingness to do something, motivating someone other than ourselves could be expressed in one of two ways:

1. Influencing someone to do what **we** want them to do

2. Inspiring someone to do what **they** want to do

It's easy to see which of the two poses the least resistance. However, let's assume that most anything to do with employees falls under the former, "influencing someone to do what we want them to do." After all, if it weren't for money, who would go to work in the first place? Sure, some people love what they do. Would they continue doing so after winning the grand prize lottery? A few perhaps. Take it with a grain of salt. This is not to say that everyone is a slave in a world of corporate dictatorship. Merely stating the fact that most people working for someone other than themselves is by definition doing something that someone else wants them to do. And so, the question we're asking is:

How do I motivate someone

to do what I want them to do?

Our default response is to use one or both of the two conventional methods: threats and bribes, fear and money.

Fear: Do your job or else

Money: Do your job, that's what I pay you for

If those methods were still as effective as they once were, we wouldn't be breaking our heads over this topic. However, in an employee's market, money and security no longer hold as much power as they did with previous generations. At best, they're just enough to get people to work with the least amount of effort possible to maintain employment. Detached and disengaged, these are the punch-in, punch-out people within your organization and they are the reason you may be stagnating as a whole. People no longer respond to threats like they used to and money, as we'll soon see, is a victim of its creation.

THE FLAW OF MONEY MOTIVATION

Many have too much, but none enough.

~ Danish Proverb ~

Ever notice how in life, there are ups and downs, and somehow, with a bit of time, things always tend to come back to normal? That's Hedonic Adaptation. Think of that raise you recently got, the new car you bought, the new girlfriend or boyfriend you started dating or the old one that may have left you. Think of someone you lost, some painful event or the time you accidentally screwed up your hair so bad you had to shave the whole thing off. Now tell me, did you eventually get over it? Did life gradually get back to normal? Did the buzz of a new car, a new relationship, a raise or new clothes eventually wear off? That's Hedonic Adaptation, otherwise known as the Hedonic Treadmill.

This tendency applies to all the fluctuations in our lives, both positive and negative. It allows us to adapt to our new environments and circumstances. In many ways, it's a beautiful thing because it helps limit our suffering. On the other hand, it's one of the factors behind our unquenchable thirst for consumerism and collection of wealth. It's quite possibly the foundation of greed and the primary reason our planet is in shambles.

Over time, we tend to devalue what we have and seek out what we don't. This phenomenon explains why money is a terrible motivator. Once you get the job or the raise, the high you get from the financial increase disappears in a short period. My clients claim it fades in two to sixteen weeks. So if you're the employer, are you supposed to give a raise every three months to keep your troops marginally motivated?

That's absurd, and you'd be out of business by the third quarter! And so, the question of motivation changes yet again to: "How do I motivate someone to do what I want them to do when money just isn't enough?"

> As we acquire material possessions, we normalize them and need something new to fill the void.

While material rewards are a must, they have their limitations when it comes to lasting motivation. If cold hard cash isn't a practical option, and reasonably so, what else can we offer someone to increase their levels of engagement? We need to find a more sustainable way to collaborate with the people that help keep our businesses alive.

IT'S NOT ABOUT YOU. IT'S ABOUT THEM.

Successfully motivating others begins with a shift in our mentality. From "what I want" to "what they want." All too often, leaders talk about their interests, their desires, and their vision. Seldom do their actions indicate a genuine concern for their employees' wishes. To those of you who may be nodding in agreement, I urge you to become aware of this common and potentially destructive behaviour. Make it less about *you* and more about *them*. Strip away the power that your title provides, humanize your approach and level the playing field. Only then can you begin to connect with your team members and create positive change.

MOTIVATION NEGOTIATION

Motivating others suggests there's a form of exchange. "I'll give you this if you give me that." A certain element of negotiation comes into play. One where mutual interests are aligned, conditions agreed upon and fulfilled by both parties.

During the hiring process, we sign an employment agreement. We exchange time, expertise and labour for salary and benefits. Employee engagement, on the other hand, isn't quite so straight-forward. There is no such thing as an agreement where someone says they'll work harder, be more focused, creative, collaborative, and involved in return for more pleasure in their professional lives. Employee engagement is voluntary. It is a natural by-product of a positive workplace that prioritizes the employee's emotional satisfaction above all else. It's about reciprocity. To receive, we must give. Aligning our interests requires us first to discover what the individual is truly after. Knowing that we are in the constant pursuit of happiness, the question of motivation finally evolves into:

> Where do people find joy at work
> and how can I help them achieve it?

We're looking for the missing links that will convert detractors into promoters and ambassadors. For the perfect combination of elements that allow us to maximize our potential. The values we seek to fulfill which render us naturally motivated and engaged

THE HIERARCHY OF JOY

Whether at work or in life, we draw pleasure from one of three categories: External, Interactive and Internal, or in other terms: Having, Doing and Being. It's a simplified way to categorize our *wants* and how they relate to the way we experience pleasure and how they correlate with one another.

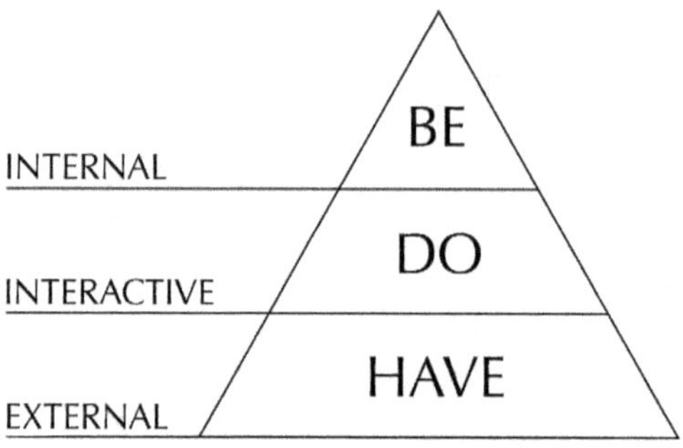

Figure 1. *The Hierarchy of Joy*

EXTERNAL (HAVING)

The first item on the ladder refers to anything in the material world such as money and possessions. The focus is on acquisition and ownership. Beyond basic human needs, our sense of fulfillment is limited by our ability to acquire these comforts and luxuries. Perceived happiness is short-lived and requires regular replenishment. In the workplace, we find examples of external rewards in our salary, benefits and other such perks.

INTERACTIVE (DOING)

The middle of the pyramid refers to any form of interaction, as in, how we experience life. There is a relationship between the individual and their environment. In the workplace, we fulfill these needs through our professional relationships and our day-to-day activities. What we do, who we do it with, where we do so and how it's accomplished.

Doing feeds *Being* and serves as a connector between the external and internal realms. The more we can interact with the outside world and be content with it by limiting our desires, the more we can extend and sustain our levels of fulfillment. For example, my motorcycle provides me long-term pleasure thanks to my interaction with it. I feel pure bliss and exhilaration when riding the open roads. The joy it brings me has lasted many years and continues to do so every time I turn the key and twist the throttle. At work, the same can be said about my plush office chair and laptop. While I might take them for granted, they provide a suitable level of comfort and productivity. All it takes is a moment of reflection to fill me with a renewed sense of gratitude and satisfaction.

INTERNAL (BEING)

The highest item on the ladder of human wants refers to our deepest selves: who we are and who we are striving to become. *Being* is the most elusive of the bunch as it brings into question, "which comes first, the chicken or the egg?" or in this case "doing or being?" For our purpose, *internal desires* refer to our thoughts, beliefs, emotions, personal growth, professional development, spirituality, personal traits, and qualities.

MOVING INTO INSPIRED ACTION

Separating our desires this way, at least with regards to employee motivation, sheds light on exciting new possibilities. Leaders who are left scratching their heads can now peer into a world beyond the conventional methods of motivation. The Hierarchy of Joy helps bring about the awareness that beyond money, there exist many other contributors to our levels of engagement at work. The advantage is not only found in the knowledge of their existence but in the fact that many of the items that fall under the *Interactive* and *Internal* realms cost much less while providing long-term, sustainable fulfillment within the workforce. Employee recognition is a perfect example. Gestures of acknowledgment and appreciation require little to no effort on behalf of the leader yet have the ability to fill the employee with a sense of accomplishment, pride, and joy.

Motivating disengaged employees is one thing. Inspiring them into active engagement and emotional investment is another. That's what we're truly after. We want to tap into the zone where the magic happens. Where creativity flows, where hours are no longer counted, where micromanagement takes a back seat, where accountability is never questioned and where everyone has a stake in the outcome.

To accomplish this, we first need to find out what drives the individual, who and why they are. Doing so reduces our dependence on material rewards. We can achieve inspiration by the overall fulfillment of not only external desires but of interactive and internal ones. Only then can we help them attain a higher form of joy by being the authentic and powerful version of themselves within the organization.

THE SWEET SPOT

POWERS. PASSIONS. VALUES.

We are usually happier doing something we're good at, something we're passionate about and something that meets our core values. Using this knowledge, we can create a personalized profile for ourselves by connecting the three most important factors that define our key motivators.

PPV Profile: Powers

Passions

Values

POWERS

NHL Hall of Famer Mike Bossy once said, "Hard work beats skill, but when elite skill works hard, you can't beat that." We're all born with a set of abilities. Things that we naturally excel at and if we were to cultivate them, we'd be able to reach levels of mastery. Some people are gifted with their hands. Some are good communicators. Some are highly creative, and some are excellent problem solvers. It's important to be able to identify these strengths because people who are great at what they do tend to be happier and more successful. It comes naturally to them and the fruits of their labour yield better results.

The great achievers we find all around us got to where they were, not only with their work ethic but with their innate talents. Focusing on what we're naturally good at points to the law of least resistance. Doing so would allow you to reach higher levels of proficiency with reduced energy investment. Do what you're not so good at, and progress will be slow and demotivating. Do what you're great at, and growth and success will come with ease.

> What are you naturally great at?

For as long as I remember, I've been in love with the sport of hockey. Growing up, I'd play on the streets with my neighbourhood friends. I strapped on my first pair of skates at the age of 12, and I've been playing regularly ever since. With such consistency and a focus on improvement, you'd think I'd be able to match up against my opponents in the old-timers league by now, but sadly that isn't the case. The harsh truth is that my natural abilities or lack thereof limit me from attaining excellence. If it weren't for the camaraderie and the need for physical activity, I would have given up a long time ago.

On the other hand, I'm a natural communicator which allows me to connect with people easily. My mind can create on-the-fly, and I'm able to express myself effortlessly. This skill has had an incredible impact on my life. Communication has always been and continues to be my bread and butter. And so, I focus much of my energies on the powers granted to me at birth. Whether it's through writing, coaching, consulting, training or public speaking, I'm always inspired and filled with joy simply because it comes naturally to me.

Identifying and tapping into your strengths and those of your employees, on its own, can generate outstanding results. It has the power to motivate, build confidence and self-esteem. It can give us a sense of accomplishment, contribution, and purpose. As a leader, there are two questions you should ask:

> What are you naturally great at, and
> how can we use your strengths to our advantage?

Within each employee exists a set of incredible abilities and limitless creativity. Help them discover their greatness and harness it in such a way that it not only energizes and inspires them to new heights but contributes to the on-going growth and success of your organization.

PASSIONS

Once we know what we're good at, it's important to infuse emotion into it. Just because we're excellent at a given task doesn't mean we want to make a living out of it.

Take for example a professional athlete that has all the skill in the world but plays with a lack of enthusiasm. You'll often hear a commentator mention during gameplay "if only player A would play with as much heart and passion as player B, he'd be unstoppable!" You can tell from the apathy, the lack of effort and engagement on the playing field that the player has insufficient passion. There appears to be a certain level of interest that just isn't there. Power without passion is like my late grandmother driving a Ferrari. So much potential, such poor performance.

What ignites you?

Before we can tap into our passions, it's important to understand what it means in this context. It isn't some fairytale feeling of glee when we think of a specific activity or cause. I prefer to look at it as anything that stirs emotions. It's easy to identify it when you hear words like "I love, I live for, or I can't get enough of…" My accountant is passionate about numbers and finding solutions for businesses. One of my best friends details luxury cars because he loves the transformation he's able to create with his bare hands. These types of passions are straight-forward and relatively easy to identify. However, some of our passions can be hiding in plain sight, and it's crucial to discover them in the workplace. Look beyond the obvious and tap into aspects of reality that move you, whether positively or negatively. We can either promote what we love or find a solution to something that gets under our skin. We're looking for a powerful emotional charge, regardless of how it manifests itself.

For instance, if you always find yourself frustrated by a lack of efficiency, this negative emotional response might point to your passion for optimizing process for increased productivity and performance. Focusing your strengths towards finding solutions to these tolerations is an excellent way to trigger a positive charge.

Passion doesn't have to be something noble; it just has to be something that ignites you. Next time you talk to someone, listen to their voice and wait until you hear an increase in emotion. Notice the moment their heart rate increases slightly, and their eyes light up. Guess what that is?

Though Power may have the ability to spark some interest, Passion is what opens the doors to motivation and supercharges us into the realm of inspiration. It's what infuses our actions with emotion, creating an unstoppable force of nature. Much like the great men and women who have shaped the course of history, every single one of us has the potential to do something amazing. By aligning our emotions with our abilities, we can begin to manifest into the formidable being we were meant to be.

VALUES

Having aligned your Powers and Passions, you should have a clearer picture of who you are, what you have to offer, what ignites you and what role you play in this game called life. There's just one last thing to check off the list before you're ready to unleash yourself: your conditions.

Values, simply put, are your list of demands based on what you deem to be non-negotiable. They are the expression of the essential things in your life. They represent your personal preferences and when combined, create your overall definition of happiness. Values act as a filtering system and help weed out any undesirable avenues. They influence the decisions and actions you take. They help us make the choices that we project will lead us towards maximum relative positivity.

For example, if you value autonomy, you might not handle a micromanaging culture very well. If you appreciate work-life balance, you won't enjoy working 60 hours a week. If you value the outdoors, you won't enjoy working in a poorly lit office. If you appreciate money, you probably won't want to work for below your financial standards.

What are your conditions?

While Powers and Passions are crucial starting points, they are impotent without Values. When it comes to motivating employees, the identification and fulfillment of their values is the name of the game. Finding out what's most important for your team members and helping them achieve their desires is the heart and soul of the process. As we'll see in depth in the following chapters, they are the primary contributors to our sense of satisfaction both, in life and at work.

PPV IN ACTION

The PPV Profile has three primary uses:

1. Finding our Sweet Spot
2. Deepening our sense of purpose
3. Matching us with suitable collaborators

FINDING THE SWEET SPOT

The PPV Profile allows us to identify our drivers and in turn, reach our highest potential. The more we fulfill and align these elements, the more we can supercharge our energies, and increase our levels of motivation beyond the thresholds of engagement and into a state of sustained inspired action. In short, we find our *sweet spot.*

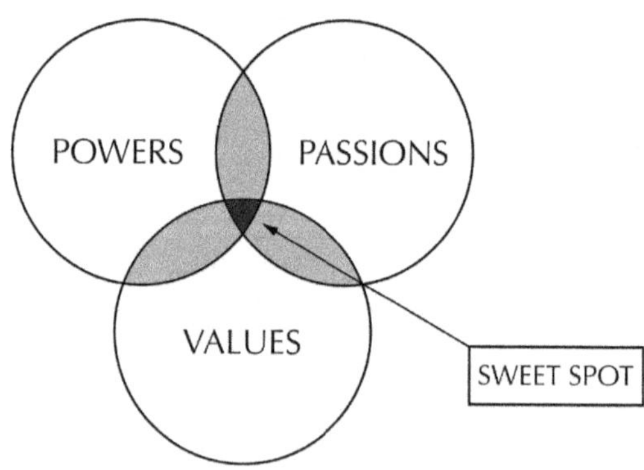

Figure 2. *PPV & The Sweet Spot*

POWERS + PASSIONS = PURPOSE

The PPV Profile is the link between profession and vocation. Identifying our Powers and Passions not only aligns us with our Sweet Spot but also helps us along in our search for Purpose, our Why. Who am I adding value to and How am I doing so? What is my usefulness? How am I contributing to the world around me?

Purpose doesn't have to be something we endlessly search for our entire lives. I urge you to simplify yours by understanding that as humans, we have a role to play just like anything else. Your pencil's purpose is to allow you to write. Your jacket is meant to keep you warm. Your phone connects you with people instantly. Your purpose needs not to be more complicated than accepting and embracing your role in this life and how you contribute to the world around you.

John Maxwell, a pillar in leadership, said: "to discover your purpose in life, ask, what am I passionate about and what am I good at?" Powers and Passions, if explored and harnessed correctly, can pave the way and allow you to feel a deeper sense of purpose. When you're great at what you do, and you're passionate about it, your purpose appears naturally. When you're in "the zone," The Sweet Spot, you rarely think twice about the who, what or how. You simply do it. You get the feeling that this is what you were meant to be doing all along. You're in your element. You're contributing your maximum potential to those around you, and your purpose will be exposed every time you use your abilities to add value to your environment. Rejoice in the knowledge that you have found your place in this universe, by actively expressing the most authentic version of yourself.

PROFILE MATCHING

Once we discover, harness and implement our Sweet Spot, we can then use the same approach to connect with those around us that share similar traits. Whether we're looking to form a business partnership, to hire an employee or to apply for a job within a company, PPV is slathered across the board. Though perhaps subconsciously, we tend to look for people and organizations that match up with our profiles. This instinct holds true for all successful partnerships. If you were to look for a collaborator, wouldn't you naturally want someone who shares common passions and values while contributing with their own set of complementary strengths?

A job interview works the same way. First, we see if the person has the skills and experience required to compliment our needs. From there, we start asking questions of introspection. If we see enough passion in their eyes, a sense of purpose in their motives and that we share common values, we are more likely to extend an offer to the candidate. Unfortunately, at times, some not-so-perfect matches slip through the cracks, and we end up with team members that are difficult to motivate. And so, if you want to have a successful team, I can't stress enough the importance of hiring the right person for the job. Having the right people on board simplifies our daily grind. It converts employees into associates, partners by your side rowing in the same direction with a common purpose: to contribute to the overall success of the team. Our mission to motivate others can only be as effective as the matching of the profiles. Otherwise, the gap to connect what you want and what they want may be too wide to merge. Once a suitable match is made, motivating and engaging employees begins and ends with the fulfillment of their personal and professional values.

CHAPTER THREE

FULFILLMENT IN LIFE

LIFE BEFORE WORK

The office space is nothing more than a designated area where fellow humans interact and work in unison to reach a common goal. We tend to get so caught up with our day-to-day that we often forget the big picture. We wake up and jump into our business skin. Then it's go-go-go until the day is over. Regardless of our title and status, we become a cog in the wheel of corporate success. To this, I say: Before work, there is life. Before life, there is nothing. It's meant to serve as a reminder that beneath all the layers, we are all human, all striving to achieve a common goal.

> Before work, there is life. Before life, there is nothing.

Satisfaction is a holistic science. One that takes everything into account, from someone's fulfillment at work and in life. An element in our personal realm may be the cause of a symptom in our professional lives and vice versa. For instance, an employee's performance may be dropping, not due to a change in their process but perhaps because they haven't slept in weeks due to their kids being kids. If we focus solely on goals and performance, we may be treating a headache with a Band-Aid. We should examine not only a problem but see the big picture: all the elements we deem essential to our overall satisfaction.

PERSONAL VALUES

Are you happy? Are you fulfilled? How is anyone supposed to answer a question that is so vague and misleading? Now try this: On a scale of 1-10, how satisfied are you with the current status of your health? How would you rate the amount of rest, physical activity and the quality of your nutrition? Now we're getting somewhere. Satisfaction is a game of balance. Fulfillment, whether in life or at work, can be better understood and defined when broken down into smaller, more focused and highly specific values. Individual categories, each with their own set of elements that make up our overall levels of satisfaction. And as you'd expect, the more these values are met, the happier the individual.

Just as your mechanic would plug a computer to your car to give you an immediate diagnosis, you can get an instant snapshot of your current levels of satisfaction, all in under a few minutes. The way to do so is to follow a two-step process:

1. Identify your values.
2. Rate your current levels of satisfaction.

The first step is already done for you. Thanks to the works of Paul J. Meyer, there's a standard set of values that have been assembled and is commonly used as an assessment tool for personal development. Industry professionals refer to it as the Wheel of Life. It's nothing more than a visual representation of the things we commonly value. Depending on which image you land on in your Google search, you may notice some variations. Some wheels have 6 or 8 elements while others have 12 or more. Some use different words while others may group or omit sections entirely. I've found that the following are more than enough to cover most of what we're after: career, finance, health, self-image, romance, family, social life, recreation, personal growth, physical environment, contribution, and legacy. Each one plays a role in our overall fulfillment. And like most things in life, it's a game of balance and wellness.

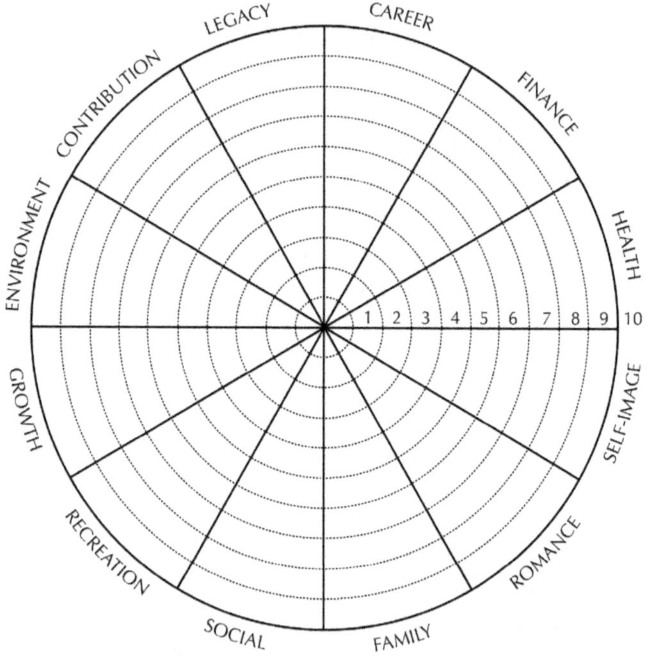

Figure 3. *The Wheel of Life*

Each of the elements can be further broken down into smaller, more personal and specific components that make up your reality. Let's take a peek into each one and explore their meaning.

CAREER

What you value in your professional world. *Career* includes the company you work for, your relationships with the people you work with, the actual job itself as well as all the other forms of rewards and stimuli.

FINANCE

Separate from career, *Finance* refers to your financial flexibility, security, savings, holdings, investments, and retirement plan.

HEALTH

This section includes your physical and mental health. Rest, activity, nutrition, free of illness and disease, disabilities and mental suffering. Anything to do with your mind, body, and soul falls under this category.

SELF IMAGE

This value encompasses everything that has to do with how you see and feel about yourself, your abilities, your appearances, and your personality.

ROMANCE

This category points to your intimate relationship with your better half. Partnership, trust, respect, acceptance, companionship, sexual activity, communication, support, and mutual values. All things love.

FAMILY

This refers to the relationships between you and your parents, children, brothers, sisters, and extended family. Those you hold dearest to your heart.

SOCIAL

This segment is about your friends and your social life. People you enjoy being around and places you like to visit.

RECREATION

This section is all about *you*. Hobbies, personal space, free time, travel, and personal possessions. Things you get to have and activities you get to do, just for yourself.

GROWTH

Growth refers to your need for learning and growing. Knowledge, personal development, experience, levelling-up, spirituality, and wisdom.

ENVIRONMENT

The physical space around you. Anywhere you *are*: your office, the inside of your car, your house, your rooms, the city, state/province, country and continent where you live.

CONTRIBUTION

Our community and the role you play in it. *Contribution* includes charitable work, donations, and philanthropy. In short, giving back.

LEGACY

This final segment is about what you'll be leaving behind when your time comes and how you'll be remembered. The words that will be spoken during your eulogy and carved into your tombstone. Connected to our quest for immortality, this is the culmination of our life's work.

PERSONAL VALUES ASSESSMENT

Once these categories are understood, give it a try and test yourself. Rate each one on a scale of 1-10, where "1" is *not satisfied at all* and "10" is *fully satisfied*. Reflect, explore and score each one. Then plot the results on the blank wheel to get a visual representation by filling in the pie sections. In a few short moments, you'll precisely know what is and isn't working to your liking. Here's a sample of what it could look like:

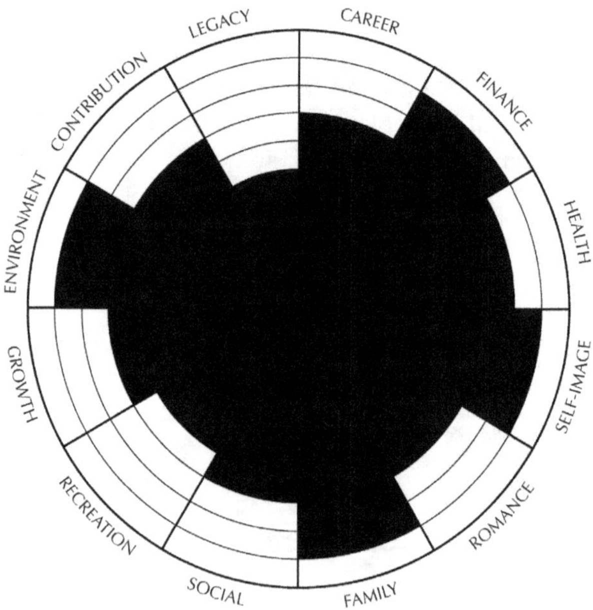

Figure 4. *Sample results*

Stand back and look at your results. Is it a full circle or is it bumpy all around? Are the sections maxed out or are some so low that it looks like someone stole a slice of the pie? Which ones are fulfilled and which ones aren't? If any, which elements need your immediate attention? How significant is each value for you? How much balance exists in your life? Your assessment should steer you in the right direction as you'll know what you need to focus on to improve your overall levels of satisfaction. The next time someone asks "are you happy?", you'll be one step ahead and know the answer inside out.

DIFFERENT STROKES

Be mindful that each category holds a different weight from one person to another. For instance, many of my clients over the age of 40 start paying attention to contribution, community, and legacy. Tweens might focus more on money, romance, and social life while people married with children emphasize the deep yearning for increased personal time and recreation. Though these are over-generalizations, it's important to understand that depending on our age, cultural background, circumstances and personality types, these values can play different roles in our lives. Additionally, our levels of fulfillment are entirely subjective and are based on the standards we set for ourselves.

The twelve elements are meant to serve as a general guideline and can be personalized. If a particular value doesn't resonate with you, remove it. Similarly, if you find a sub-value is important enough to have its own category, then go ahead and create it. The idea is to build a wheel that represents you. One that reflects your current reality and your ideal life.

DIGGING FOR GOLD

Within each category, we can find relative sub-values. When assessing your results, it's a good idea to explore each section and identify precisely where there's a lack of satisfaction. For instance, you may have a low score in Family, but it may be one specific thing that is skewing the result. Perhaps it's a verbal dispute you had with a sibling or maybe your in-laws come over too often. Another example could be that your general physical and mental health is good but find you lack sufficient rest. These 12 categories are general guidelines. It's up to us to dig deeper and discover what's causing a lack of fulfillment. More importantly, once we find the cause, it's our responsibility to take immediate action and improve our reality. Our happiness depends on it.

While personal values play a crucial role in our lives, the primary area of concern for leaders is found within the Career section where we uncover our professional values. Following this path will lead us to the elusive land of employee satisfaction and engagement.

CHAPTER FOUR

SATISFACTION AT WORK

CAREER VALUES

Wouldn't it be nice if we could take the guesswork out of motivating employees? If we had a list of highly specific things we generally look for in a job, then we can use it to gauge our current levels of satisfaction. A set of metrics that can provide both the employee and the leader with real-time data. Information that can be used to identify and attain objectives with the sole purpose of increasing fulfillment and engagement at work. To accomplish this, we'll need to explore the Career section from the Wheel of Life. Doing so would supply us with a preliminary set of six career values:

CAREER VALUES OVERVIEW

1. Organization
2. Compensation
3. Responsibilities
4. Relationships
5. Mind & Body
6. Self-Esteem

These six categories encompass the things we typically deem most important in our professional lives. They're the principal factors that make for a happy worker, and each has a corresponding segment in the Hierarchy of Joy.

The following illustration shows how they line up with our External, Interactive and Internal desires.

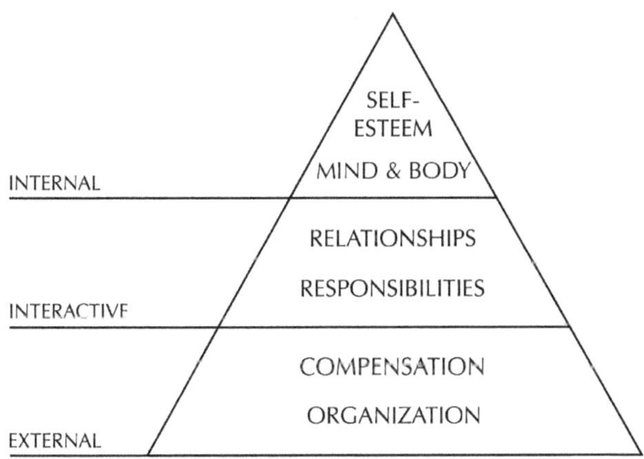

Figure 5. Career Values & the Hierarchy of Joy

As we continue to expand these segments, we ultimately end up with a comprehensive grouping of all the elements that contribute to our overall levels of satisfaction. Unlike other business metrics commonly used, Career Values aren't meant to determine productivity, performance or profits, but instead, the emotional state of the workforce. A tool we can use to finally move away from a vague "how happy are you at work?" to a highly specific "what is and isn't working for you and how can we improve?" The fulfillment of these values paves a direct path to increasing employee engagement which in turn, improves performance and productivity while reducing absenteeism and turnover. Not by force, but by choice.

CAREER VALUES: THE COMPLETE LIST

ORGANIZATION

- Products & services
- Vision & mission
- Physical environment
- Culture & values
- Employee feedback

RESPONSIBILITIES

- Nature of tasks
- Variety of tasks
- Workload
- Autonomy
- Tools & resources

MIND & BODY

- Learning & development
- Challenge
- Creativity
- Stress
- Health & wellness

COMPENSATION

- Salary
- Benefits
- Vacation
- Flexibility
- Stability

RELATIONSHIPS

- Trust & respect
- Collaboration
- Communication
- Feedback

SELF-ESTEEM

- Job Title
- Accomplishment
- Contribution
- Recognition
- Purpose

ORGANIZATION

Aligning yourself with the company you work for is something that should be taken into heavy consideration before you start your first day. This element, External in its nature, is often difficult to influence. Although a company would be wise to collect and be open to employee feedback and suggestions, fundamental changes to the essence and culture of the business are hard to come by. This inherent inflexibility is why the interview process is vital. It's meant to identify candidates that align with the organization from the start. When choosing to join an organization, or when hiring someone, ensure that you/they:

- Appreciate and endorse the products and services.
- Are aligned with the vision, and mission.
- Are aligned with the organization's culture and values.
- Are satisfied with the physical environment, be it within the office space or the geographical location.
- Understand and are aligned with the openness to employee feedback and organizational improvement.

COMPENSATION

Nobody likes to be shortchanged. This section is all about the rewards you receive for keeping up your end of the bargain and being a productive worker. Although this sits nicely in the External segment of the pyramid, there could be some room for negotiation and controllability. The usual suspects are salary and benefits, but also includes vacation time, flexibility in the schedule for life's unexpected demands as well as the level of stability and security the job offers.

RESPONSIBILITIES

As we transition into the Interactive realm, this category focuses on the job itself. How you use your mind and your body to serve the organization. Your day-to-day responsibilities. *What*, *how* and *how much*. It's what you signed up for when you agreed to be employed by the company. We not only accept to execute the work but to take on everything that comes with it. Here we explore the nature and variety of the tasks, the workload, the tools and resources provided and the level of autonomy.

RELATIONSHIPS

We spend over 40 hours a week at work. By default, this means we potentially spend more time with our co-workers than anyone else. These relationships make up a large portion of our daily interactions and can directly affect our levels of engagement. Enjoy who you work with, and you can do any job with a smile. Dislike them, and even the most pleasant task will become painstakingly undesirable.

Explore each group of people you work with, be it your leaders, peers, colleagues, employees, and clients if applicable. To simplify this process, we'll split this segment into two categories: your leader and your peers. For each grouping, inspect the level of trust and respect, collaboration, communication, and mutual feedback. Relationships are at the heart of the Interactive segment, and as such, we all have the power to create a positive outcome.

MIND & BODY

As we shift towards Internal desires, we turn our focus on our mental and physical wellness. We need to stimulate our minds with continued learning, on-going development, and professional growth. Humans are naturally creative problem-solvers. We crave new and exciting challenges where we can use some of our inventive creativity to overcome these hurdles. Most importantly, we need a good balance. Achieving mental and physical wellness requires manageable stress levels and a healthy work environment.

SELF-ESTEEM

The most profound of the Career values, Self-Esteem refers to who we are and how we feel about ourselves. It is highly personal and tops off the pyramid's Internal section. It doesn't matter what you do for a living, if you don't feel good about yourself, you won't be at your best. While materialistic in its nature, a job title works wonders to feed our confidence. Delving a little deeper, we find the elements that satisfy our senses. Those of accomplishment, contribution, recognition, and purpose. We want to know that our work makes a difference, that we play a role in the overall success of the organization. Mostly, we want to feel acknowledged and appreciated, feeding our natural need for acceptance and validation.

CAREER VALUES ASSESSMENT

Just as we did with the Wheel of Life, we can now take a snapshot of our current levels of satisfaction in our professional lives. The purpose is to gain clarity and point to the areas that may be in need of improvement. You can use this tool as a self-assessment, either on your own or with an unbiased certified coach. If there's enough trust, use it as an exercise during one-on-ones with your leader or employee. To the extent, you can use it as an anonymous survey throughout your organization which would provide it with valuable feedback.

INSTRUCTIONS

1. On a scale of 1-10, rate your current levels of satisfaction for each value in the list, where "1" is *not satisfied at all* and "10" is *fully satisfied*.

2. Optional: On a scale of 1-30, rank each value by their level of importance to you, where "1" is *the most important value* and "30" is *the least important value*. One number per value so that each number is used only once. The idea is to sort them by order of importance.

3. Plot and analyze your results.

CAREER VALUES ASSESSMENT

VALUES	SCORE	RANK
ORGANIZATION		
Products & services	/ 10	/ 30
Vision & mission	/ 10	/ 30
Environment	/ 10	/ 30
Culture & values	/ 10	/ 30
Employee feedback	/ 10	/ 30
COMPENSATION		
Salary	/ 10	/ 30
Benefits	/ 10	/ 30
Vacations	/ 10	/ 30
Flexibility	/ 10	/ 30
Stability	/ 10	/ 30
RESPONSIBILITIES		
Nature of tasks	/ 10	/ 30
Variety of tasks	/ 10	/ 30
Workload	/ 10	/ 30
Autonomy	/ 10	/ 30
Tools & resources	/ 10	/ 30

RELATIONSHIP - LEADER

Trust & respect	/10	/30
Collaboration	/10	/30
Support	/10	/30
Feedback	/10	/30

RELATIONSHIP - PEERS

Trust & respect	/10	/30
Collaboration	/10	/30
Support	/10	/30
Feedback	/10	/30

MIND & BODY

Learning & development	/10	/30
Challenge	/10	/30
Creativity	/10	/30
Stress	/10	/30
Health & wellness	/10	/30

SELF-ESTEEM

Title & role	/10	/30
Accomplishment	/10	/30
Contribution	/10	/30
Recognition	/10	/30
Purpose	/10	/30

TOP 15 VALUES BY RANK

You can use the following grid to plot your results.

1. List your top 15 values in order of importance.

2. Rate your current levels of satisfaction for each one.

3. Assess the results and, if desired, repeat the exercise for the following 15 values.

VALUES BY RANK	SCORE
1. _______________________	/10
2. _______________________	/10
3. _______________________	/10
4. _______________________	/10
5. _______________________	/10
6. _______________________	/10
7. _______________________	/10
8. _______________________	/10
9. _______________________	/10
10. _______________________	/10
11. _______________________	/10
12. _______________________	/10
13. _______________________	/10
14. _______________________	/10
15. _______________________	/10

ANALYSIS

Now that you've plotted your results, what stands out for you? What are you learning about yourself and the organization? Remember that, depending on the person, some of the elements may be more significant than others. It's also entirely possible that new values emerge. The key is to maintain flexibility and to draw from the assessment what you may. Focus primarily on your highest ranked values as those are the ones that contribute most towards your levels of overall satisfaction.

SUM OF ALL VALUES

There's a deep connection between the PPV Profile, the Wheel of Life and the Career Values and they are all naturally linked to our Common Denominator. Each tool serves its specific purpose towards the fulfillment of our ultimate goal. While independent of one another, together they make up the sum of our definition of success and happiness, both in life and at work.

I encourage you to pause here for a moment and imagine that all of your Career Values were fully met; that you were 100% satisfied in all aspects of your professional life. How would that affect your world within and beyond the office walls? In this ideal state, we're drawn to conclude that not only would we be happier but highly engaged and inspired. We would jump out of bed energized, eager to take on the challenges that await us. Our intentions and actions would never be questioned. The need for micro-management would evaporate as we would be highly autonomous, having claimed complete responsibility and ownership over our results and desired outcomes. Our interests would be in perfect alignment with those of the organization. We'd experience a cultural shift towards coaching and mentoring. Our work would be a seamless extension of the company's vision, mission, and values. Not by force or duty, but by free will, driven by our natural pursuit of happiness.

FACILITATING GROWTH

Understanding all the elements that contribute to our overall levels of satisfaction is a vital step to inspiring positive change. As leaders, equipping ourselves with this awareness allows us to facilitate fulfillment in others. The happier the people within your organization, the more engaged they'll naturally be. Grasping the principles of human motivation and professional values is a giant leap forward. The second half of the journey is in the execution, as in, "how do we accomplish all of this?" The solution is found in the art and science of leadership coaching.

CHAPTER FIVE

LEADERSHIP COACHING

WELCOME TO COACHING

I absolutely believe that people, unless coached,
never reach their maximum potential.
~ Robert Nardelli ~

Coaching is a partnership. It can supercharge people's potential by harnessing their strengths and desires, by aligning them with highly specific goals, strategies and action plans, and by supplying them with a healthy dose of accountability.   The reason it's so effective is that it allows the coachee to dig deep within and become self-aware. Being coached enables us to tap into our deepest values and helps us better understand ourselves, our desires, our patterns, and the motives behind our actions.

Coaching can be as straightforward as microwave popcorn yet as complex as reading this book backward and upside down. John Whitmore described it best when he wrote: "Coaching is unlocking a person's potential to maximize their growth." Understanding its purpose is as simple as reading this quote yet masterful execution can be as tricky as humanizing artificial intelligence. It's a realm where science meets art, where logic meets emotion, where silence and presence can be more impactful than a thousand words and where trust is more powerful than any force of nature.

Coaching isn't only about a method that facilitates growth. It's also a way of being, a way of communicating and a way of creating awareness. It has a way of bringing the best out of people which in turn infuse their positive emotional energies into their daily actions. It isn't a coincidence that so many highly successful people all over the world have coaches. If celebrities, athletes and CEO's use them, then perhaps it would be wise to offer these benefits to the everyday men and women that make up our organizations and communities.

Coaching has changed my life. It has transformed the way I communicate, it has helped me discover who I am underneath all the layers and it has allowed me to help others in ways I never knew existed. The lens I use to see the world has evolved in such a way that I no longer recognize my old self. I judge and impose my opinions less. I listen and understand more. My clients claim the same results, which is why I firmly believe that it can do the same for you. As for the workplace, the effects are just as astonishing. The research lines up perfectly with my clients' testimonials and they're as follows:

Benefits of Coaching:
- Develops leadership skills
- Empowers team members
- Increases efficiency
- Improves time and stress management
- Enhances decision making and goal setting
- Develops communication skills
- Promotes positive relationships and collaboration
- Encourages buy-in and increases engagement
- Nurtures creativity and reduces power hierarchies
- Improves attitude and team morale
- Boosts employee retention

These benefits confirm my belief that this is something every company needs to adopt if they haven't done so already. Every a-ha moment, every obstacle overcome, every employee that's been given a new lease on their professional life, every leader whose daily grind is converted into effortless motion and every quarterly report that provides proof of steady improvement chips away at the old to reveal the new, positive, more successful version of your organization.

QUALITIES OF A LEADER-COACH

Coaching is a human approach. Beyond the "doing" of it exists the "being" of it. As such, before jumping into the act of coaching, we should first explore some of the qualities that will help us along. Developing personal qualities isn't something we accomplish overnight. It's not like learning how to program your new phone or file your taxes. It's about changing who we are by reprogramming years of conditioning and by modifying behavioural habits. It requires a strong willingness, self-awareness, focus and time. Qualities aren't objectives to be attained and forgotten. They are fluid and evolve just like the weather and our moods. Sometimes we have it, and sometimes we don't. It's about maintaining mindfulness and a relentless desire for self-improvement.

Take a moment and look through the following list. Notice the words that describe you and those that need some improvement. Observe and absorb what you may. If any words are missing for you, go right ahead and add them. I tend to regularly check this list to see how it resonates with me. The key is to keep chipping at the old to reveal the new, improved version of ourselves.

COACHING QUALITIES

Patient	Confident	Likes to help
Honest	Tactful	Light-hearted
Flexible	Inspiring	Good role model
Present	Authentic	Nonjudgmental
Creative	Motivating	Understanding
Intuitive	Empathetic	Able to connect
Curious	Trustworthy	Open to not knowing

Having gone through this list, can you agree that these would be some of the general traits you would want out of your leader? What words are missing that you'd like to add? How would your own life and leadership style change if you improved some of the qualities above that you may be currently lacking? How would this affect your relationships at work and home? If ever you veer off-course, pull out your list, take a moment and realign yourself. Humans aren't perfect nor are we meant to be. The idea is to increase self-awareness in the quest for personal development.

THE THREE PILLARS

Coaching is comparable to most healthy relationships. They both require ethical behaviour and mutual consent. A solid bond built on trust, respect, and an efficient way to communicate with one another. The only difference is that, in coaching, there is a methodology behind it. Combining the elements above helps us gain a better understanding of what coaching is and how to go about *doing* it.

PILLARS OF COACHING

1. Positive relationships
2. Effective communication
3. Coaching structure

POSITIVE RELATIONSHIPS

Whether we're looking to improve our leadership skills or to coach our employees, there is nothing more important than laying down a solid foundation. By that I mean, building positive relationships with the people around us. What would a company be without them? The concepts of teamwork, collaboration and success cannot exist without people getting along, trusting and relying on each other. Same goes for coaching. Whatever the objective, if someone other than yourself is involved, you must aim towards creating a strong connection with your partners.

EFFECTIVE COMMUNICATION

A partnership serves little purpose unless everyone is on the same page. Once we've established a solid bond, it's essential to use a method of communication that will increase the level of mutual understanding. The words we use have a tremendous impact on the quality of our relationships. Therefore it's crucial to gain knowledge on all the things that occur subconsciously between silence and noise, between listening and talking.

COACHING STRUCTURE

The main difference between coaching and the typical relationship is that there is a method to the madness. A framework to work around. Some form of structure that can serve as a set of instructions that we can follow to ensure that both the leader and the employee are getting the most out of the time they're spending together.

CHAPTER SIX

POSITIVE RELATIONSHIPS

EFFORTLESS COLLABORATION

Before we can engage in conversation, be it a one-on-one for coaching, partnership, offering feedback or attempting to resolve a problematic situation, we first need to agree to collaborate. Call it cooperation or active participation towards reaching a common goal. The objective is to entice the person in front of you to act as an ally. We want to encourage them to drop their guards, join forces and eliminate resistance willingly. To accomplish this, we need to state our intentions and ask for permission. The formula to remember is the following:

$$I + P = A:$$

Intention

Permission

Agreement

INTENTION

State your intention clearly and honestly. Doing so helps eliminate any possible reservation the person may have. It helps increase trust with transparency, encouraging them to drop their guards and to be open to what you want to accomplish. In the event where you'll be coaching a team member, explain what you're trying to do and what your limitations are on your expertise. Most importantly, disclose the purpose behind your intentions.

PERMISSION

Empowering others with choice is the name of the game. Moving ahead without permission is like trespassing on someone's property. Chances are you won't feel very welcome. If you wouldn't hang out in your neighbour's yard without an invitation, what makes you think you can do so in the interpersonal realm?

Titles form hierarchies. The idea of having a status of dominance over another lays a trap. Leaders forget that permission is about respect, regardless of circumstance. Level the playing field by offering them the ability to choose. A simple "are you ok with that?" should suffice in everyday dialogue. Here's a sample of how the two go hand-in-hand:

> "Hi Maria, I know that we haven't been very cooperative lately. My intention today is to try to resolve our differences and get back on track to where you and I can start working together again, as a team. I know it hasn't been the case in the past, but I want to be more supportive of your initiatives. Would you be ok with hashing this out with me?"

How do you think Maria would respond to this gesture? You're essentially asking her for help to resolve a mutual problem. Success is a team sport and using the I+P=A approach is the key to effortless collaboration. Easy to understand. Easy to apply. There should be no reason as to why you couldn't put this into practice as of this very moment.

AGREEMENT

There are three possible responses to your request. It can be a straight-up yes or no, or they can negotiate. Such as "I'd like to hash this out with you but maybe now isn't the best time. Can we schedule a meeting sometime this week?" Regardless of their response, you'll have your answer, and the decision is entirely up to the other person, empowered with choice and flexibility.

Once you have permission to proceed, do so with caution. Positive relationships are the building blocks of any great organization. The success of the whole depends on your ability to build and maintain them. They are fragile and require your attention to detail. If you're able to keep the same level of trust, respect, and courtesy in the verbal interactions that follow, you'll soon find yourself surrounded by allies and positive relationships.

TRUST IS EVERYTHING

Trust is the glue of life.

It's the most essential ingredient in effective communication.

It's the foundational principle that holds all relationships.

~ Stephen Covey ~

Let me be abundantly clear on this: without trust, there can be no great leadership or coaching. Most everything we aim to accomplish in our professional lives relies on some form of human interaction. Therefore, our ability to connect with those around us is of utmost importance. When it comes to coaching others, the relationship depends entirely on our ability to explore deeply, rendering the process as effective as possible. If there's a lack of trust, many essential elements could be missing in the conversation. Information that is not only vital for gearing the ship in the right direction but for tapping into the nucleus, the person's truth.

Establishing trust should be your starting point and the foundation of your endeavour. It's about creating a safe and supportive space built on respect. It's about showing genuine concern for the person. It's about integrity, honesty, and sincerity. It's about being authentic and non-judgmental. It's about establishing clear agreements and keeping your promises. It's about holding your coachee's words in your vault, in full and unbreakable confidentiality. It's about your code of ethics and how you uphold it. It's about believing in your coachee, even if they don't do so themselves. It's about asking permission and empowering them by relinquishing all hierarchy.

Whenever a leader comes to me with a set of challenges in coaching their team members, the relationship or lack thereof tends to be the root cause and establishing trust, often the primary solution. Once there's a strong bond, all it takes is a genuine desire to help a person, and the results will come naturally.

BE HONEST

Nothing destroys trust faster than deception. Whether we do it intentionally or not, the outcome remains the same. Being honest and transparent shows that you have nothing to hide. It tells others that they can proceed without fear and that they can approach us without reservation. Honesty stems from authenticity and security, from knowing ourselves and our deepest intentions.

WALK THE TALK

Align your actions with your words and uphold your agreements. Trust is gained when we are reliable and somewhat predictable in our behaviours. People generally don't like surprises. Brushing along the lines of deception, the unknown pushes people away from those who lack consistency. When you give your word, be true to it.

BE VULNERABLE

Humanizing ourselves does wonders when it comes to building trust. The act of removing our masks, relinquishing our egos and levelling the playing field eliminates hierarchies. This nakedness deepens the relationship as transparency, authenticity, and honesty are at their primal level. Allowing others to see our imperfections makes them feel better about theirs. No titles, no hierarchies, no pride. Merely humans experiencing this crazy thing called life, together.

BE A VAULT

The ability to keep other people's secrets holds incredible value. Psychotherapists and lawyers, among other professionals, take an oath to uphold this principle. Certified coaches are no different. That's because nobody wants to give out highly sensitive information to a double-agent. Eliminate the urge to gossip. When people trust you with their stories, keep it in your vault. This safe place should only have two keys: yours and theirs.

MAKE IT SAFE

Trust is nothing more than an extension of our need for safety and is rooted in our instincts for survival. Create a safe space for others with acceptance and respect. Being nonjudgmental, understanding and caring helps build a resilient bridge. Resist the urge to be critical by embracing the imperfection that comes with being human. Show them that there is absolutely no risk when engaging with you.

BE IN THE MOMENT

Realize deeply that the present moment is all you will ever have.
~ Eckhart Tolle ~

Is there anything more frustrating than talking to someone who isn't listening? Ever been in a team meeting where some people are chatting or playing on their phones while you're trying ever so desperately to get your point across to deaf ears?

Leaders don't have much time to spare. We're scrambling to put out fires. We're running from meeting to meeting. We're planning, designing and executing strategies and action plans. We're always on the clock and time is usually not on our side. We tend to become excellent at multitasking, and though it's valuable to the fruition of the projects at hand, the human octopus tends to fall short in one area: the ability to turn the motor off and be truly present.

Presence on its own can transform how you communicate with those around you. It's a sign of respect, of caring about what the person is trying to say. Additionally, it allows you to catch onto the titbits that aren't being said but felt. It's what will enable you to tap into your intuition. It's what tells the person in front of you, "I'm 100% here, present and listening. For the time we've allotted, there is you and only you. You're the only thing that matters at this very moment." Great leaders know that above and beyond many other motivators, their time and undivided attention is the currency for a highly engaged workforce.

CHAPTER SEVEN

EFFECTIVE COMMUNICATION

BETWEEN SILENCE AND NOISE

The art of communication is the language of leadership.

~ James Humes ~

No two humans are alike, and as such, no two individuals can fully understand each other. We each have our way of seeing the world. We use different lenses and belief systems. We have different opinions and perceptions based on our backgrounds and experiences. And so, if we are to communicate effectively, we must do everything in our power to connect our worlds.

Effective communication is a way of interacting such that mutual understanding is maximized, paving the way for a deeper connection and improved collaboration. There exists an array of elements between silence and noise. We use them daily yet we might be unaware of their existence and their impact on our conversations. They can be visualized on the following illustrations.

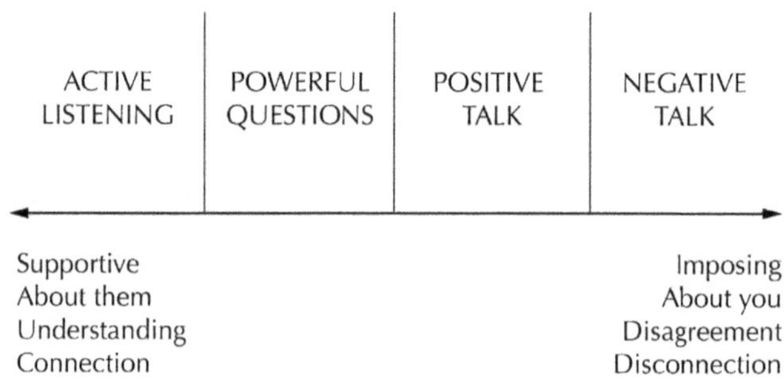

Figure 6. *The Spectrum of Communication*

Three primary pieces make up effective communication, and they are active listening, asking powerful questions and using positive talk. By limiting ourselves to within this range, we ensure that the focus is on the person ahead with the intent of understanding each other. The spectrum of communication can range from being harmless and constructive to risky and potentially damaging. From being supportive and understanding to imposing and in disagreement.

EFFECTIVE COMMUNICATION

1. Active Listening
2. Powerful Questions
3. Positive Talk

In contrast, delving into negative talk brings us into murky territory as we talk and impose our will on others. Here is where we discover the source of most negative interactions, leading to arguments, disagreements and the possible deterioration of relationships.

Communication breakdown is often at the heart of disagreements. Arguments may arise out of a sheer lack of understanding and can cause a tremendous amount of frustration, lost revenue and productivity. When I'm called upon to offer advice, opinions or suggestions, tips on effective communication is often where I start and finish. A lack of expertise on the topic is widespread. Whether it is accomplished by increased awareness, education or breaking down over-inflated egos, this hurdle must be overcome at all cost. Effective communication is a crucial competency for leaders and coaches alike. Applying it to your daily interactions can single-handedly alter your relationships. Its potency is why you'll find a variation of this concept in any profession where communication is vital.

ACTIVE LISTENING

When you talk, you are only repeating what you already know.

But if you listen, you may learn something new.

~ The Dalai Lama XIV ~

We can sometimes make the simplest of things into painstakingly difficult ones. Listening is the epitome of this reality. All it requires is your presence and your undivided attention on the information being transmitted to you. However, the challenge of quieting our minds, resisting the urge to judge or reply immediately in agreement or disagreement seems to be a constant saboteur. It's as though we are on an endless quest to be validated, to show that we too share the same issues, that we have all the answers or that we so firmly believe in our truth that there can be no other possibilities. Perhaps it's because we are so emotionally attached to our thoughts, beliefs, perceptions, and opinions that we end up identifying ourselves with them.

GO BEYOND WORDS

Albert Mehrabian is best known for fuelling the debate on verbal versus non-verbal communication. Though possibly through slight misinterpretation, his work has come to be known as the 55-38-7 rule. It states that 55% of communication is body language, 38% is the tone of voice, and 7% is the actual words spoken. We're not here to debate the percentages and occurrences. What we do know for sure is that it isn't all verbal.

Active listening goes beyond merely hearing the spoken words. It engages the listener to focus on the speaker in a way that would help them understand what is being expressed. The difference is like hearing a song played in the background versus listening to it attentively, loud and clear. Paying attention to each musician's part that makes up the symphony. The beat the drummer has chosen to keep the rhythm with the bassist. The choice of chords the guitarist uses to express the emotion in the song. The lyrics the singer uses to convey a message, not just with words, but with melody and emotion. There is so much that goes into writing and performing a song. A connoisseur will be able to decipher messages well beyond an amateur could ever dream of comprehending. Just like *getting* a song, understanding each other requires just as much focus and attention to detail. What is being said and not said? What is being communicated through words, tonality and body language? Are you interpreting the message exactly the way it was intended? And even if you are, how would you know?

BE PRESENT

Be fully immersed in the moment, turn on your radars and go on high alert just like you would when playing a video game or watching a riveting movie. You want to be ready for any subtleties that may come your way. Free of distractions, there is nothing more important than what is being communicated in this very instant. Before engaging in conversation, consider taking a moment to clear your mind of any worries or lingering thoughts. An express meditation is my go-to before all my meetings and sessions. No more than 5 seconds is all that's required. Breathe in. Breathe out. Ready, set, go.

LISTEN ATTENTIVELY

Hear everything that is being said and not said. Keep an ear out for keywords that stand out, words that may point to a more profound message. What are you hearing? Do the tone, energy, and tempo accurately represent the words they're using? Are there any words that stand out for you? Is there an underlying theme to the conversation?

FOLLOW YOUR GUT

What isn't being said, but felt? Beyond your ears, what do you see and feel? Tap into your intuition and go beyond the obvious. What is your gut telling you? Is there something beneath the words? When you ask someone "how's your day" and they respond by saying "fine" but their body language says they're going through a rough spell, you know they aren't "fine."

Be mindful that the bulk of communication hides beneath the surface. Our mission as the listener goes beyond merely processing words and accepting them as the entirety of the message. If your gut says that something's wrong, then chances are you're right. Trust your instincts.

ALLOW ROOM FOR EXPLORATION

One of the reasons I have my own personal coach is to help me achieve clarity. That's because even though I consider myself an excellent communicator, I don't always know what it is I'm trying to say. How's that for a curveball? When people talk, it's entirely possible that they don't know what it is they're trying to communicate. The act of listening creates room for exploration. It allows the speaker to express themselves out loud and to explore their topic in greater depth. Be aware that this may very well be the case and provide the speaker with some space to explore and gain clarity.

ENCOURAGE THE FLOW

When someone talks, we usually and often subconsciously encourage them by using both verbal and non-verbal cues. We nod and tilt our head in agreement. We use words like "mm-hmm," "go on," "really," "and," "I see," "yup." Have you ever noticed yourself doing so? The reason is that we want to encourage the speaker to continue talking and to let them know that we are listening. It's about acknowledging what they're saying without interrupting. It's about creating a space where the speaker feels like their message is important and that the listener values what they're attempting to communicate.

CLARIFY, REFLECT, SUMMARIZE

So far, we've been listening, absorbing, deciphering, sensing and encouraging. There's just one last step in becoming a pro at active listening, and that is to make sure that what the speaker is saying is what we're understanding. It's time to talk. Not to reply but to clarify. It's time to touch base and connect the dots. We want to bridge the gap between the speaker and the listener. We want to make sure that the message is accurately received. We want to avoid making assumptions and strive towards complete understanding.

Clarify what's being said, eliminating all ambiguity in the message. Reflect the content, feelings, and meanings to the listener by paraphrasing or repeating what's being said or felt. Sometimes echoing one keyword back to the person can be enough to unpack more baggage and to propel the conversation forward into further exploration. Be a mirror and provide a measuring stick of how well you're understanding each other. Bring to light what's being transmitted either verbally or non-verbally, consciously or subconsciously. Summarize the conversation, especially when dealing with multiple stories and topics in one sitting. Tie everything together and reframe the content into one, nicely wrapped package. In short, we want to clarify, reflect and summarize what we hear, see and feel.

Though we may be *talking*, we're not adding anything new to the conversation. We are deepening the understanding, helping to create heightened awareness and providing perspective. Active listening is quite possibly the most powerful yet underestimated tool we each have access to when it comes to interacting with others.

POWERFUL QUESTIONS

To ask a powerful question is to ask one that the answer isn't readily available. It's to challenge someone to go into introspection, into self-discovery mode. It's a question that encourages the person to pause, think and reflect. To explore their thoughts and emotions and to discover something they may or may not have known about themselves. It's to ask a question that will benefit the individual, create perspective and encourage understanding. Powerful questions stimulate and awaken. They provide insight and clarity. They reveal desires and objectives. They are open-ended questions driven by active listening. They help create forward momentum in the conversation. They are less about a topic and more about the person and how they relate to it. Powerful questions, like active listening, stem from a state of curiosity and positive intentions.

ASK OPEN-ENDED QUESTIONS

Contrary to closed questions which are answered with a dry "yes" or "no," open-ended questions leave room for exploration and reflection. They encourage the person to dig deeper by formulating longer answers. They also help steer the dialogue in new directions as the answers may open doors to uncharted territory. Open questions encourage both parties to go into a realm of discovery. Closed questions can be converted to open ones by replacing those starting with "can," "could," "should," "is" and "do" by "what" and "how."

BE CURIOUS

Following your curiosity is the best way to construct powerful questions. Rather than prepare a session with preset ones, curiosity allows you to be in the moment. People tend to think of an answer while the other person is talking. Following your interest in the speaker encourages you to quiet the mind, to listen attentively, to absorb and better understand the message. There is no such thing as the perfect question. Trust that with curiosity and your intuition, these questions will emerge naturally, in a steady state of not knowing and wanting to find out.

KEEP IT SIMPLE

Avoid asking multiple questions stacked into one. Take a moment to formulate your thoughts. When ready, ask a short, concise question. The simplest inquiries are often the most thought-provoking ones.

USE THEIR LANGUAGE

We are more open and responsive when we are most comfortable. Human connection relies on our ability to find common ground. Therefore, consider using a language and tone that reflects the person's words, style, and personality.

PRACTICE PATIENCE

Embrace and acclimate yourself with the potential discomfort that comes with silence. Listen completely, without interruption. When the person finishes answering, wait. A follow-up answer can be hiding behind the wall of silence and patience is the key to discovering it. The first answer often creates awareness within the speaker which in turn might give birth to a second, more profound and meaningful response.

INTERRUPT MINDFULLY

Human's tend to be great storytellers. While good around a campfire, this creative and wandering aspect of our minds can also veer a dialogue way off track. If ever the person goes into storytelling, respectfully interrupt and realign the focus back to the topic at hand. Ask them how the story connects to the topic-du-jour, regroup and move forward.

BEWARE OF "WHY"

Be mindful of the effects of asking "why" questions as they can only be answered with a "because..." Doing so automatically puts the person in defence mode requiring them to justify themselves. Consider replacing "why" questions with "what" or "how" questions. For instance, "why did you do this?" could be reformulated as "what was your reasoning behind this course of action?" This approach has less of a judgmental feel to it and gives the person some breathing room to explain their thought process.

BE CAUTIOUSLY FEARLESS

Powerful questions are a great way of challenging an employee. Without being confrontational, it's essential to be fearless in your questioning. Your ability to do so can create an opportunity for increased self-awareness and open doors to new possibilities.

LISTEN. ASK. REPEAT.

We can summarize masterful communication in two words: *listen* and *ask*. If you only practiced these two things, the way you communicate and interact with others will transform before your eyes. Your professional and personal relationships will improve, conversational tensions will disappear, the energy will take on a positive spin, and people will love to talk to you because you're great at listening and asking questions. They'll feel listened to, appreciated and respected. Next time you interact with someone, follow these steps: Listen. Ask. Repeat.

POSITIVE TALK

There's a difference between talking and telling, between offering and imposing. It's the contrast between objective feedback and criticism, observation and judgment. The key to talking is to use words in such a way that they will have a positive impact. We want to add value to the conversation without injuring the person. Whether your input is received as positive or negative depends on how you deliver it.

Do you impose your opinions and advice on others or do you offer it as a suggestion? Do you jump in to solve other people's problems as soon as you get the chance to or do you allow them space and support to get creative and find their way? As leaders, we're conditioned to put out fires and to fix problems. When our team members approach us, we find it easier to give away the answers rather than take the time to mentor and empower them; to help them become autonomous. Unless it is a matter of urgency, where time is a factor and action must be taken immediately, there is no need to bark orders. My expert opinions and advice rarely become the solution my clients are seeking. That's because everyone has their own set of circumstances and set ways of going about doing things.

From team meetings to one-on-ones, it's crucial to be mindful of this and to refrain from emotionally attaching ourselves to our ideas. Accept that there could be a better way to solve the same issue. Be aware that imposing our will only lead to power hierarchies and negative interactions. The humble leader is one who acknowledges the creative powers in others and is open to the idea of not knowing. Be eager and willing to learn and grow from the snippets of wisdom lingering in the minds of all those around them.

OPINIONS AND ADVICE

Offering opinions and advice should be an option of last resort, once the person has exhausted all avenues and possibilities. When they've hit a brick wall, step in and offer a helping hand to give them a boost to overcome their challenges. Offer it as a suggestion, as a gift without attachment. When in doubt, ask permission. Empower them with the choice to either accept what you're offering or to discard it.

ME TOO

When listening, we often hear a voice in our head that screams out "me too!" It stems from our natural urge to find common ground. Resist this temptation and refrain from jumping in with your story that might overshadow theirs. Instead, keep it in your back pocket. If ever you feel that your experience can serve as a source of learning and expanding the conversation, use it. Timing is everything. Allow the person to extract from it what they will. A piece of wisdom often emerges from knowing that someone other than ourselves shares our struggles and has walked the path before us.

A WORD ON APPRECIATION

Whether we have the authority to move mountains or none whatsoever, we can and should always resort to using the powers of appreciation. There is no cheaper, easier, quicker and effective way to encourage and motivate people than by showing honest appreciation. Recognizing the achievements of your workforce creates an environment of positive reinforcement, providing your team members with an instant sense of accomplishment, acknowledgement, and gratitude. This one simple gesture is often the difference between having a happy, engaged employee and one that is discouraged and ready to walk the plank.

WRAPPING UP

In time, using effective communication will solidify your professional and personal relationships. It's the key to tapping into the greatest resource your organization has, the people that make up the workforce. Embrace it. Use it to your advantage. Tap into the limitless creativity and motivation that's hidden within your walls and discover how great the people around you can truly be. If ever you're in doubt about your skills in effective communication, remember to start with a state of curiosity, positive intentions and follow the rule of thumb: Listen. Ask. Repeat.

THE GPS MODEL

COACHING STRUCTURES

All roads lead to Rome, but our antagonists

think we should choose different paths.

~ Jean de la Fontaine ~

Establishing deep human connections and masterfully executing the art of effective communication, together make up a large portion of the coaching puzzle. The missing link is how to go about doing it. To engage in a relationship where the goal is to maximize someone's potential requires some form of structure. A set of instructions to get through a one-on-one where the goal is to promote learning, growth, accountability, and success.

There exists an array of coaching structures, many of which are nearly identical in methodology. If you want to know how many different coaching models exist, find out how many books are written on the topic and you'll have your answer. Coaches, like leaders, like to find their own, unique way of looking at the process and put their personal touches on them. The truth is, there is no definitive structure. Only suggested guidelines. Regardless of the method you adopt, you'll find common benchmarks that tie them together. Elements and markers that differentiate a coaching session from an everyday conversation.

Few leaders want to explore and expand their abilities into professional coaching. Most want just enough to get the job done. Chances are you have enough on your plate which is why efficiency is of utmost importance. It's for this reason that I'll be introducing you to the following method which contains the bare essentials to get you going.

THE GPS MODEL

The best way I found to describe the coaching approach is by using the following analogy: Coaching is similar to your GPS. The awesome little device helps you get from where you are to where you want to be. It consists of a three-step process most of us are already know:

1. You enter your desired destination.
2. You explore a range of possibilities.
3. You select your desired path and go.

The GPS coaching model follows this same pattern.

GPS Model: **Goals**

Possibilities

Selections

This logic is essentially how coaching works. If you want to help someone reach their objective, you first need to know what it is that they want to attain. Once set, you can explore the options and select a course of action. The GPS coaching model is a simplified method that includes identifying the Goal, exploring the Possibilities and Selecting an action plan. Consider it a cheat sheet, a quick go-to reminder of what to be aiming for in your one-on-ones. However, each step needs to be expanded and thoroughly understood.

Even though you might have a GPS on board, there are many other requirements to get to your destination. As in, do you have a car? Do you know how to drive? Do you have enough fuel? Do you know where your pit stops are and if you have access to roadside assistance? What time are you taking off? How will you know you've arrived? Do you have what it takes to get there? More importantly, are you sure that's where you want to go?

As straight-forward as the process may seem, we must explore each step in-depth. We must ensure that our employees have everything they need to succeed. Doing so maximizes the potential for success, and it's the purpose of the coaching model. It lays down some parameters that help direct a conversation into one which focuses on a specific objective. It steers the interaction in the direction of positive momentum and the attainment of concrete results.

IDENTIFYING GOALS

This first step in the GPS Model is the heart of the process because, without a destination and a motive, we are directionless and purposeless. Therefore, before moving on, there must be a clear topic to address, a centrepiece around which the entire conversation will work around. We're not concerned about action plans. We're first trying to understand their desires, their goals, and their motives.

> *What Do You Want and Why Do You Want It?*

The purpose is to identify and explore one topic, one objective that will serve as a reference point for the session. Not just the *what* but the *why*. Anything and everything to do with the vision of success comes into play, including the motives behind the desire. As we'll soon find out, the answer to the question "what do you want?" may land anywhere between our ultimate desires and all the way down the ladder to the tiny, baby steps to achieving it: process goals and action items.

Above all else, we want to make sure that what they want is what they *really* want; that the person's goal is directly or indirectly connected to their definition of success. Doing so ensures that they'll be motivated enough and committed enough to see it through. Setting a goal we don't actually want to achieve is like driving to the ice cream shop when we really want a slice of pizza. A waste of time and energy. Our role as their leader-coach is to make sure that the goal is something that there is a burning desire to achieve or at least a relatively important reasoning behind it.

I spend a considerable amount of time helping my clients figure out what they truly want. That's because we often don't know what that is. We might have an idea but to hone it down into something highly specific is not always in our DNA. As leaders, it's our job to help them discover those answers. Once we've created awareness, once the *what* and *why* are defined, the *how* automatically unravels. The script practically writes itself. We are naturally creative, highly resourceful problem solvers. However, to tap into these abilities, we first need to create the ever-elusive and deeply satisfying a-ha moment, otherwise known as creating awareness. We need to flip the switch that makes their eyes light up, fills them with positive emotion and gets them eager to tackle whatever is standing between them and their objective.

THE BIG PICTURE

Goals are rarely standalone and are often interconnected with another. Above each one is a higher motive and beneath it, a method to achieving it. One feeds the other creating a vast network linking our pursuit of happiness with our daily actions. If we were to stand back and get a bird's eye view of it all, we'd see the big picture.

Goals nourish values, the sum of which contributes to our broader sense of fulfillment. The reverse also holds true. Within our definition of joy, we find values. Within values, sub-values. Within sub-values, goals. Within goals, processes. The big picture is the unification and global sum of our values, objectives, and actions. When identifying goals, the *What, How* and *Why* are the navigation tools required. Together they not only help pinpoint the objective but paint the big picture.

> **What**: What do you want?
>
> **Why**: What purpose does it serve?
>
> **How**: What is required to achieve it?

Once a goal is defined using *What*, we can dissect it into smaller chunks using *How*. Inversely, following *Why* helps us understand the reasoning and how it connects to the common denominator.

In the following illustration, we can see the correlation between these types of goals and how we can navigate up or down the ladder. For the sake of simplicity, we'll use the terms Large Goals (LG), Medium Goals (MG), Small Goals (SG) and Process Goals (PG). These tags aren't meant to imply size, rather one's relation to the other.

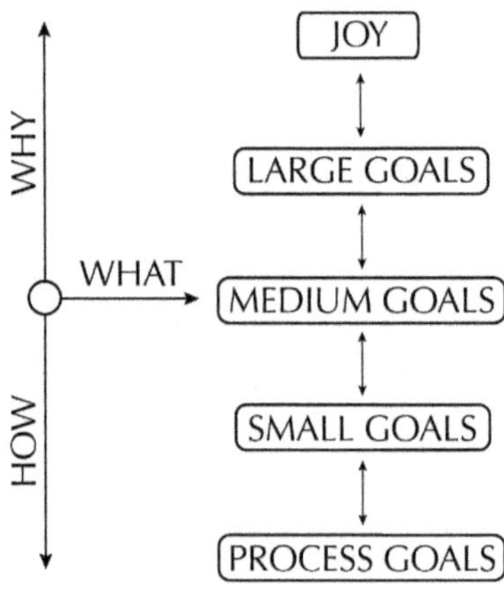

Figure 7. *Flow of Goals and Motives*

Each instance where why is asked elevates the reasoning by a notch until it reaches the deepest motive, the overall definition of success and happiness. Each time the how is asked, it explores the process further until it is broken down into specific action items to be carried out. Please note that this isn't to suggest that we can only experience joy once a larger goal is met, but rather how our reasoning works with regards to our goals and motives.

To put this into perspective, here's an example of the flow created by repeatedly asking *Why* and *How* type questions.

WHAT: "I want to be healthy."

WHY:

- "I want to be healthy because it'll strengthen my body."
  - "A stronger body allows me to live a longer life."
    - "Living a longer, healthier life will make me happy."

In this example, exploring the motive behind "wanting to be healthy" connected this primary objective with the hope of living a longer, healthier life. Attaining this higher objective is linked to the ultimate desire of being happy. We now know exactly why this person wants to be healthy. Let's now go in the other direction. Using the same objective as the starting point, let's dig into the process and see how the objective can be attained.

HOW:

- "To be healthier, I could exercise regularly."
  - "I can exercise regularly by joining a yoga studio"
    - "In order for me to join, I have to call the studio."
      - "I'll do that today."

Exploring *How* helped generate some possibilities. It linked *being healthy* to exercising, from exercising to yoga and finally from yoga to the specific action item of calling the studio and signing up.

Our minds already work this way when breaking down goals into smaller action items and when connecting our desires with our motives. However, unless we are mindful and put it into practice, we might not look at our fulfillment in such a large format. Being able to link our goals, motives, and process into one interconnected vision of success lets us get a broader view of the person's world. Reflecting this back helps increase clarity and perspective. Once we understand how everything fits together, we can then start putting the pieces of the puzzle together. It might also help to visualize the Big Picture as a tree diagram.

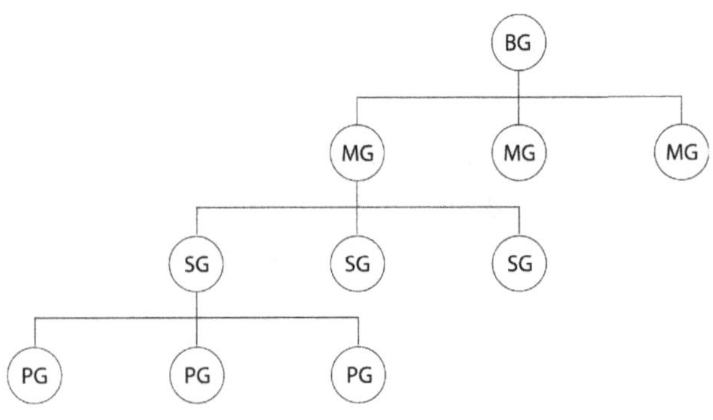

Figure 8. Tree of Goals and Motives

Each goal can be broken down into smaller fragments, building blocks, reaching the point of granular action items. For each Big Goal, you may have multiple Medium Goals, multiple Small Goals, and multiple Process Goals. Each one plays a part in achieving the next level up, ultimately allowing us to reach the overall satisfaction we're after. The *What, Why* and *How* are relative, inseparable and virtually the same. Every single one of them is a goal in itself.

GOAL EXPLORATION QUESTIONS

Below you'll find some sample questions that can help get you started. There is no specific order or starting point. Wherever you find yourself, naturally navigate until you define the goal. Once done, create a mental map of the vision of success by following the Why and How. When satisfied, choose a direction for the day. Ensure that there is one specific topic for the session. Doing so will increase the focus and the probability that the person leaves with something concrete. Trust that your presence, creativity, and curiosity will take care of developing your own set of powerful questions. What and when to ask is entirely in your hands. Remember to let the employee lead the way. It's their agenda, not yours. Be the co-pilot and help them get to where they want to be. Where they get to choose the *What*, *Why* and *How* of it all.

Sample Questions:
- What do you want?
- What question do you want to address?
- What is the vision of success?
- What do you want to discuss today?
- What is so important about this goal?
- How does achieving it add value to your world?
- What will it enable you to do?
- How does it fit into the big picture?
- What do you want to walk away with today?

GOAL GENERATORS

We are living in times of practically limitless choice. Asking someone "what do you want?" could trigger analysis paralysis, a blank stare, not knowing how to answer the question. As a leader-coach, one of our challenges is to help others identify clear objectives. To reach the desired destination, you first need to know where you're heading. Without a subject to focus on, there can be little to no coaching. If ever you find yourself in such a predicament, take comfort in knowing that there are plenty of great ways to generate one.

ASSESSMENTS

Using self-assessments such as the ones included in this book (Career Values and the Wheel of Life) or any other performance-based ones, are an excellent place to start. These self-evaluations provide a defined set of menu items, a list of predetermined and flexible themes to work off. Wherever you find a low score, you'll find a topic worth exploring and, if desired, an objective worth attaining.

FEEDBACK

Direct, constructive and objective feedback offers real-time information can feed the meeting. It gives us a glimpse through an outside lens. It can help shed light on our blind spots by providing us with an external view of our behaviour and performance.

CHALLENGES

Coaching can have a problem-solving element to it. Identifying difficulties and roadblocks is the most natural way of generating an objective. Helping someone overcome a given challenge is inherently part of the process. Whenever one arises, it automatically feeds a coaching interaction as though one went hand in hand with the other. The presence of a problem insists that a solution exists. Use this duality to your advantage by using the coaching approach as a way to close the loop and to help you employee find the answers they seek.

NEGATIVITY

Internal negativity is caused by a misalignment between our internal and external world. It is a mismatch between our ideals and our reality. In other words, what we have doesn't meet what we want. It's our mind and body's way of letting us know that something is out of whack.

> Internal negativity is caused by a mismatch between our ideals and our reality

This misalignment is all around us. You can find it in losing a job or being passed up on a promotion. It happens when getting a speeding ticket, gaining unwanted weight, coming in second place in a race, burning your toast or spilling wine on your white shirt. They are all events that are contrary to our ideals and expectations. Any time you sense some negativity, be mindful that it's due to this gap.

Coaching in itself is a way of connecting the external and the internal. Aligning the two is the foundation of the approach: "what do you want and how can you achieve it?" The entire idea of *wanting* is based on the concept of *lacking*. If you wish to improve your romantic life, chances are something is missing in it. If you want more money than you currently have, it's because you don't feel as though you have enough of it. If you want a better job, you might be unfulfilled with the one you already have. These desires often manifest themselves as negative emotions and expressions. No different from a baby crying for mother's milk. That's great news for the coach in you because wherever you find negativity, beneath you'll uncover a topic to tackle and something worth coaching.

CONVERTING NEGATIVITY

Though the source of negativity is in the misalignment of expectations and reality, the actual cause of the emotional turbulence is in our inability to influence the outcome. In many instances, the concept of control is a false and misleading one. We tend to want things that we have no influence over. Regardless, it is imperative not only to identify the source but to claim responsibility and focus on the controllability of the matter. With this knowledge, we can convert negativity into a potentially self-controllable and attainable goal by following a four-step approach.

C4 Method:	Complain
	Claim
	Challenge
	Convert

STEP 1: COMPLAIN

The first step is to identify the source of the negativity. It's time to let it all out and express whatever is lingering inside, pointing to the misalignment between ideals and reality. It's easy to recognize a complaint as it's usually external, negative and outside of our control.

Sample Questions:

- What's the complaint, the problem?
- What are you currently tolerating?
- How is this affecting your life?
- What's the default outcome if nothing changes?
- Why do you want to address this? Why now?

STEP 2: CLAIM

Once the source of negativity is voiced and identified, it's time to gain awareness of its counterpart: our role in the matter. This step often reaps instant rewards because it creates a shift in the mindset by challenging the individual to change their viewpoint. From looking outward to reflecting inward. Claiming responsibility for our circumstances has a disarming effect. The negative energies begin to drop as the level of awareness rises. You'll find the language here changes from "he," "she," "they" or "it" to "I."

Sample Questions:

- What role do you play in the matter?
- How are you allowing it to happen?
- Which choices led you to this predicament?
- What part of this do you control?
- What are you pretending not to know?
- How are you convincing yourself otherwise?
- How are you disempowering yourself?

CHALLENGE

Once the negativity is at bay and the focus has shifted inward, it's time to identify the real challenge, the obstacle that needs to be overcome to resolve the matter. I've found the best way to accomplish this is by filling in the following sentence.

"With regards to this situation, I am unable to __________ ."

The words used to complete this line must be something the person controls, be it their actions, their thoughts or their attitude towards the given situation.

CONVERT

The last step in the process is to flip the switch, from negative to positive. We can accomplish this by replacing the challenge with a desire. From "I am unable to____" to "I want to be able to____." For instance,

"I *am unable to* communicate my needs."

becomes

"I *want to be able to* communicate my needs."

A goal is often nothing more than negativity that is rendered self-controllable. The C4 Method should equip you with some tools to help convert it into a highly specific, self-controllable and achievable goal. One that can feed your coaching sessions and can be facilitated using the GPS approach.

EXPLORING POSSIBILITIES

Once you enter your desired destination, your GPS calculates your current location and supplies you with options. It can compute the journey based on your mode of transportation. It takes into account traffic spots, accidents and construction zones. It even provides you with a trip duration and time of arrival. In short, it tells you how you can get there.

What Can You Do?

The word *can* is what we want to focus on. The key is to be void of bias, negative self-talk, considerations, challenges and roadblocks. Outside-the-box thinking and absolute creativity, I find, is what opens the floodgates of possibilities. Options we may have never thought of before. Shortcuts and workarounds that may be hidden in plain sight. As a leader-coach, we must them step out of this box, to look at the topic with a fresh perspective. We must create a safe space for creation and exploration. The idea is to generate as many options as possible. Explore every potential avenue to achieve the desired outcome. This is where brainstorming with a dry-erase marker and a whiteboard may come in handy. Here are some questions to help you with uncovering possibilities:

Sample Questions:

- What can you do to achieve this?
- What are all the options?
- What else can you think of?
- What are you leaving off the list?
- What strengths and abilities can you rely on?
- What resources do you have readily available?
- Who can you ask for assistance?
- What strategies could increase the probability of success?
- What are you hesitating to consider as an option?
- What past successes can you use in this situation?
- How could you go about doing so?
- What information is missing?
- How can you inform yourself?
- What advice would you give someone in your shoes?
- Who else might have been in this same predicament and how did they go about solving it?

Ask questions that will help broaden the exploration of possibilities. If your employee runs out of ideas, chime in with some suggestions or personal anecdotes that might contribute positively to the dialogue. As always, ask permission to do so. I highly encourage you to adopt the following line: "May I offer you a suggestion?" Once granted, offer it without attachment. As a gift. Nothing less. Nothing more. They could either accept it, refuse it or most likely, use it as a catalyst for new ideas to emerge.

SELECTING A COURSE OF ACTION

You've helped your employee gain awareness. You've identified one or more specific goals, mapped out a vision of success and established an objective for the one-on-one. You've tapped into their deeper motives and explored all the possibilities. All that's left is to select a desired course of action.

What Will You Do?

This final step is a decision, a commitment to a specific, executable and self-controllable task. Before you seal the deal on an action item, there are a few things to consider.

SPECIFICITY

We must leave little room for assumption or interpretation. The higher the specificity, the higher the likelihood of success. Failure to do so is like entering nothing more than a country as a destination into your GPS. With no address, city or state, it's hard to imagine you'll get to where you want to be. The same goes for our objectives and action plans. The who, what, when, where and how should be clearly defined.

Furthermore, ensure that the goal is measurable. As in, how much and by when. Success relies on our ability to gauge progress. Otherwise, how will you know you've achieved it? Hash out all the details and set a timeframe for the action plan. If in doubt, narrow it down to a specific date and time. With a highly specific target set, we're able to make a precision strike with pinpoint accuracy.

CHALLENGE CHECK

There's no use setting ourselves up for failure. Often we get so excited to conquer whatever we're after that our eyes want to eat more than our mouths can chew. Like someone who wants to get back into shape and decides to change their lifestyle overnight. They commit to working out seven days a week only to realize that they're unable to do so.

We're better off taking smaller, more attainable steps. Ask "On a scale of 1-10, how difficult or challenging is this for you to accomplish?" If the answer is anything above an 8, renegotiate the action plan. Otherwise, it could have a discouraging and frustrating effect, leaving behind an abandoned objective.

COMMITMENT CHECK

There's a big difference between what we could and should do, and what will do. We want to know how motivated they are, that they'll be loyal and dedicated to seeing it through.

Similarly to the Challenge Check, you can ask "On a scale of 1-10, how committed are you to completing this?" If the answer is anything below an 8, you may want to renegotiate. The goal or the motive may have to be revisited. A new plan may have to be designed. You may even come to find that the objective isn't what they wanted all along. If that's the case, don't get discouraged. It's all part of the process of learning and growing, just another step towards increasing awareness.

FLEXIBILITY

Jeff Bezos hit the nail on the head when he said: "I think you can be stubborn on your vision but flexible on the details of how you get there." Along those lines, it's a good idea to render the action plan flexible. Think of it as a counter-strike against Murphy's Law. Our ability to adapt to the changes and unforeseen circumstances is often what allows us to reach our goals. Remaining flexible and having contingency plans provide a "what if" scenario along with options to counter such an occurrence. For instance, if the goal is to print a report every afternoon at 4 pm, an alternative could be to do it the following morning. Flexibility allows us to have a fail-safe in place, giving us a healthy margin of error.

Sample Questions:

- What will you do specifically?
- Exactly when will you do it? Date and time.
- Who is involved in this action plan?
- How will you go about doing it?
- How much of it will you do?
- On a scale of 1 to 10, how committed are you to getting this done?
- On a scale of 1 to 10, how difficult is this to accomplish?
- What is your contingency plan?

ENDING THE SESSION

Hopefully, by now, you're both energized by positivity and gratitude for the time spent together. You've covered all the bases including the Challenge and Commitment Check.

Now's a good time to recap the session. You can ask your employee to summarize the action plan to ensure they know exactly what needs to be done. I also like to spend a few minutes as a cool-down period to remove my coach's hat for a moment and touch base as a fellow human being. To wrap up the session, ask "How was the session for you today?" and "What's your takeaway?" Doing so helps sum up the experience and the new learnings. Once the meeting is done, don't forget to thank them for sharing their time and information with you.

FOLLOW-UP

Accountability is the glue that ties commitment to the results.

~ Bob Proctor ~

Maximizing someone's potential doesn't start and stop with a coaching session. It's a relationship built not only on trust and a focus on growth but of accountability and support. As such, follow-ups are a valuable part of the process. It's about continued loyalty to reaching the objective.

Before jumping on to a new topic in the following session, touch base and assess the results from the previous one. We want to inquire about the successes, the new challenges, and learnings that may have occurred. Acknowledging and identifying the transformation helps create momentum and increase self-confidence. It encourages responsibility and progress. It also helps accelerate the coaching process.

It's always a good idea to supply them with a set of questions that encourage preparedness on behalf of the employee which facilitates flow and efficiency in-session. A coachee that comes in ready with a topic to address could save both parties a great deal of time. Otherwise, you'll be spending precious minutes trying to identify a goal and questioning the effectiveness of coaching altogether. Hold them accountable for being prepared. A fruitful interaction depends on it.

Sample Questions:

Since our last meeting,

- What was accomplished?

- How was it experienced?

- What were your top successes?

- What challenges did you face?

- What did you learn about yourself?

- What new challenges emerged?

For our next meeting,

- What topic do you want to discuss?

- What is so important about it?

- What is your desired outcome for the session?

- How can I adjust my approach to better suit your needs?

Proper reflection and preparation before a session dictates the direction and sets the tone. Constructively utilizing every minute of the one-on-one is paramount to exploiting its benefits. The responsibility lies solely on the employee to pull their weight, to carry out their action plans and to provide a topic. We must hold them accountable for the sake of their growth and continued development.

CYCLE OF GROWTH

Learning and growing is the result of a three-step process. It consists of creating awareness, taking action and assessing the results. Rinse and repeat. It's the principle of trial and error. As a leader-coach, it's our role to help the employee gain awareness, identify objectives, select and execute action plans, and assess the results.

Figure 6. *Cycle of Growth*

The cycle starts with heightened awareness. A desire is born, and a goal is identified. The coaching process goes through its movements culminating in specific action items. In between sessions, the employee executes the plan. They accumulate new information and understanding. Increased knowledge about themselves, their patterns, their process, their performance, their motives, their perceptions, their reality, and their given objective. The results are assessed, and the cycle starts anew. In the following session, either a fresh topic is brought to the table or the old one is revisited for further exploration.

CHALLENGES OF THE LEADER-COACH

The old saying "It's easier said than done" definitely applies to coaching in the workplace, especially when carried out by leaders with their team members. Establishing pillars such as building trust, intimacy, creating a safe space and overcoming bias is precisely that, easier said than done.

LACK OF EXPERTISE

A leader may or may not have the know-how to be a competent coach. They may not have basic training, coaching qualities or competencies. There may even be a lack of interest in using the methodology altogether.

Consider the following:
- Does the coaching approach interest you?
- Do you welcome feedback and self-improvement?
- Are you willing to invest time and effort into it?
- Are you open to being coached?
- Do you have a desire to learn and grow?
- Are you ready and willing to contribute to the continued development of your team members?
- Are you open to the idea of not providing answers and remaining in a state of curiosity, of *not knowing*?

LACK OF TRUST

Ideally, in a coaching relationship, there's a voluntary buy-in as well as an opportunity for the employee to select their coach of choice. Finding the right fit is crucial to a powerful partnership. However, in the workplace, the employee doesn't get to choose who their leader is and therefore, doesn't get to choose their coach. Topics may remain superficial due to a lack of trust, a conflict of interest, a fear of expression, a fear of the outcome or quite simply a personality mismatch.

Consider the following:

- What is your relationship with your coachee?
- How much trust is there between the two of you?
- What agreements do you need to put in place?
- How can you increase the level of trust?

BIAS

The leader has a dual role to play. One, the leader and the other, the coach. It's important to differentiate and communicate when switching hats. Stating your intention and asking permission helps put both parties in the right mindset. Be mindful of the following challenges:

- Difficulty in switching roles from leader to coach
- Emotionally detaching from the topic
- Remaining unbiased and nonjudgmental
- Resisting the urge to chime in with opinion, advice, unwarranted feedback or give orders

TOPIC LIMITATIONS

Employee empowerment is about giving them the ability to choose their objectives. However, a leader may feel that their role is to identify the goals, creating predetermined topics for the sessions. This leaves the employee with nothing more than the ability to explore possibilities and select a course of action to satisfy the needs of the leader. While useful when setting expectations and performance-based goals, the employee should otherwise be granted the freedom and creative power to identify their desired objectives.

GO HYBRID

There is no doubt that equipping leaders with fundamental coaching skills can completely transform your organization. On the other hand, it does come with its set of challenges. To counter this, consider using a hybrid strategy: In-house leader-coaches and external unbiased, certified ones. This two-pronged approach would simultaneously provide teams with inspirational leadership as well as a professional support system.

WRAPPING UP

The ability to build positive relationships, communicate effectively and coach employees, together can change the culture within your walls. They help us better understand each other, why we do the things we do and where we find pleasure in our personal and professional lives. They help create accountability and support. They challenge us to not only help others but to strive towards our continued development and growth.

To become a leader-coach, we must first be coached ourselves. To influence positive change in others, we must first experience this transformation within us. Every rung on the leadership ladder should embrace their evolution. Peer-to-peer coaching serves this very purpose. A process that focuses on helping each other, in collaboration and selfless in its intentions. One that encourages all members aboard to row in the same direction. Each person as valuable as the next, interconnected in unified vision and purpose. As a community, working together to achieve the overall success of the organization.

CHAPTER NINE

THE NINE CONDITIONS

NINE CONDITIONS FOR SUCCESS

I make a mean cup of coffee, if you give me the right ingredients.
~ Ice Cube ~

Success, in some form or another, is often our primary concern. Whether we're aiming to build a house, increase our earnings, improve our performance or simply make a mean cup of coffee, we're forever trying to accomplish something. While certainly diverse, they all have the same requirements to come to fruition. The Nine Conditions for Success unites these essential principles and serves as a guideline to help you achieve your objectives, regardless of their nature. When setting goals, either for yourself or your employees, ensure that they meet these requirements.

THE NINE CONDITIONS FOR SUCCESS

1. You must gain awareness

2. You must take charge

3. You must know what you want

4. You must know why you want it

5. You must be able to control it

6. You must be willing to pay the price

7. You must commit to it

8. You must believe in yourself

9. You must take action

CONDITION #1: YOU MUST GAIN AWARENESS

Before we can want something, we have to be made aware of its existence. As we perceive, we observe and judge. We compare our ideals with our current state, and then it clicks. "I must have, do or be this, that or the other!"

A black car is washed more frequently than any other. That's because dirt is more apparent on black than on other colours. My wife's car doesn't last a day whereas mine could go a week without needing a wash. Why is that? They surely both have the same amount of dust and dirt accumulation. The only difference is the contrast. Black paint makes the dirt pop. The colour of the car, nothing more, creates the need for constant cleansing.

Awareness is the Big Bang of all objectives. Without it, there can be no progress as there is no objective to attain. A blind man will never need to change the colour of his walls just as a deaf person will never need to adjust the volume of the television. Sensations, perceptions, and observations feed our awareness which in turn fuel our desires. Without awareness, there can be no success because there's no starting point and no destination. The objective doesn't exist.

This first condition is often self-fulfilled yet without it, there would be no need for change. Look no further than our current shift toward environmental preservation. Scientists all over are bombarding us with their findings with the hope of creating this awareness. Call it enlightenment or a shift in consciousness, humanity's endless quest for survival and self-improvement starts and ends with it.

CONDITION #2: YOU MUST TAKE CHARGE

You must be ready and willing to take charge of your life and your goals. You have to claim complete ownership and full responsibility for your success. Complainers and blamers gather around. Pushing your problems and sorrows onto the backs of others will get you no closer to your objective. It disempowers you and slows you down. Relying on the world to make our dreams a reality is downright delusional. Name your goal, climb the mountain and plant your flag at the top. Claim ownership over what you want and rely on no one other than yourself to bring it to fruition. This is not to say that you can't partner up but rather to be accountable for the results.

There's no *how* in claiming responsibility. It's a decision, a choice you make. Your happiness is your responsibility, and the day you own that truth is the day your world will change for the better. Take comfort in the knowledge that this is well within your grasp, that it takes nothing more than a flash of enlightenment and a life-changing decision to nudge you onto a path that will reignite the fire in your heart.

CONDITION #3: YOU MUST KNOW WHAT YOU WANT

As we saw in the GPS model, the more you can specify a goal, the more likely you are to hit the bullseye. It's the difference between wanting to be happy and wanting to increase your physical activity by joining your local running group. The latter is a clear and precise objective while the former, relatively directionless and without a specific destination. Similarly, when you go to a restaurant, and the waiter comes by to take your order, do you say "please bring me food"? I somehow doubt it. You say exactly what you want, "a double-cheeseburger, hold the onions, with a side of fries and a root beer." The game of success works the same way. A lack of direction, not knowing what we're truly after is the number one blockage when it comes to moving forward, towards a better, more desirable outcome. There is no fixed destination. It's just an idea, a dream, and a vague one at that. You can attach any title or description to my coaching practice, but the absolute truth and reality is that my primary focus is to help people answer this one tricky question: "What do you want?" And while awareness opens up a world of possibilities, exploring and identifying the goal is the key to attaining precisely what it is that you seek.

Additionally, failure to do so before launch could prove to be a waste of your time and a source of frustration. Think of the people you might know who spent years studying a field only to find themselves in a career they detest. Before embarking on your journey, do you know what it is that you want? Can you see it, smell it and taste it? Can you envision it? Ensure that you can describe it in such detail that you could write an entire page about it in full colour.

CONDITION #4: YOU MUST KNOW WHY YOU WANT IT

Even though this condition is fourth on the list, it could very well be the first and only item. Do you know why you want it? The *Why* is everything. It feeds all the other elements. It empowers the *What* with deep reasoning and motive. It's what ensures that what you want is what you really want. It's what will guarantee that once you reach the goal that you will bask in the glory of it rather than be disappointed once at the top. It's what keeps you driven through the ups and downs of the process. It's what connects your emotions with your actions, your heart with your body. It's what puts the fire in your eyes and what ensures that you'll outwork your competition. It's what connects your objective to your ultimate one of attaining maximum pleasure, maximum joy.

If you want to know if your *why* is supercharged, check to see how closely related the attainment of the goal is to your definition of joy. The closer the relation, the more reasoning behind the action. The higher the objective on the Hierarchy of Joy, the closer the connection to your deepest motive. How many degrees of separation is there between what you want and what you believe will make you happy? Connecting your *what* with your *why* renders success, not a matter of *if* but *when*.

CONDITION #5: YOU MUST BE ABLE TO CONTROL IT

We only have power over a few things in life, and it's dictated by our mind and our body. Whether or not you get the results you want is dependant on your influence in the matter, your response to a given circumstance. This isn't meant to be a limitation to what you can and cannot achieve. If anything, it challenges you to focus on what you do control and let go of what you don't.

Setting a goal that is outside of our control is a recipe for failure. You can't dictate whether you win the lottery or not. You can, however, choose to buy a ticket. If your goal is to win the lottery, you might be disappointed. If your goal is to participate regularly, then you have what it takes to succeed, not to win the prize but to be eligible to do so. This is why the process is more important than the result. The process is all we can commit to. It's what we can influence and contribute to the achievement of our objectives. To that, I say "focus on the process, not the goal."

When presented with a difficult situation, it's good to remind ourselves of the powers we actually command. The naked truth is that, barring disabilities, the only things we control are our mind and our body. The things we do, say, think and believe. This includes our attitude towards a situation and our ability to accept what we cannot change. All too often we forget this fact and place our expectations on our ability to alter things beyond our control. This pattern is what helps create unnecessary negativity within.

Body: What we do and what we say.

Mind: What we think and what we believe.

These may not seem like much but remember that there is a nearly infinite array of combinations available to us. How we use one or more of these abilities can influence whether or not we achieve our desired outcome. Being mindful of this also determines whether we allow an adverse event to affect us negatively. When there's nothing more we can do, all that's left is to decide whether or not we're willing to accept it for what it is. A lot of our negative emotions sprout from our inability to influence and attain our desired results. Whatever the predicament, ask: "what do I control in this matter?"

CONDITION #6: YOU MUST BE WILLING TO PAY THE PRICE

Everything has a price tag. There are no exceptions. Every *yes* we say means we're saying *no* to something else. The grander the desire, the heftier the price. I've come to refer to this as "potatoes and rice, you have to pay the price." The reason I use this peculiar line is that whenever I'd commit to starting a fresh, new project, I'd end up spending the ramp-up period doing just that: eating potatoes and rice. While perhaps an over-exaggeration, the steep cost attached to our deepest desires are very real. Without a willingness to making sacrifices and hard commitments, a bold decision fizzles away as quickly as it is imagined.

Once you've set your sights on the target, take a moment and check the tag. What's the price you have to pay to achieve it? Is it money, time, work, energy, focus, compromises, overcoming fears? What does it cost and are you willing to fork it over? Your willingness to pay the price for what you want often dictates whether you pursue an objective or not. The higher your motive, the higher the desire to move forward and pay the piper. When setting your goals, ensure that you're able to make the sacrifices required for achieving success.

CONDITION #7: YOU MUST COMMIT TO IT

Commitment is the name of the game. We must stick to the process and see it through. Otherwise, no matter how brilliant the idea, it will never see the light of day. Like a book half-written or a house without a roof, without commitment, you'll never reach your destination. It's about completion, rooted in dedication and loyalty. It's the very definition of finishing what you started, staying on course until you get to where you want to be. Success and commitment are interconnected. One cannot exist without the other.

If you want to succeed, you must overcome the peaks and valleys that come with the adventure. You must have the patience and give the process the time and space it needs to come to fruition. Planting a seed, alone, won't give you a crop. It requires water, sunlight, oxygen and time. Similarly, commitment to the process from beginning to end is an absolute requirement.

Setting goals that are realistic and exciting is a great way to ensure that you'll stick to it. Your *what* supercharged with your *why* should keep your juices flowing. However, even the most passion-driven objective can fall prey to the obstacles in your way. This is why it's necessary to break down the bigger goals into tiny, easy to achieve objectives. Setting benchmarks and challenges to manageable levels help build momentum and confidence, ensuring that you'll neither get bored or frustrated. The strategy should be one that energizes and inspires you every step of the way.

CONDITION #8: YOU MUST BELIEVE IN YOURSELF

Henry Ford said it best with his quote "Whether you think you can, or think you can't - you are right." Success starts within the mind, with a positive attitude and an unshakeable belief in your abilities.

Beyond the land of mystics, there exists a genuine link between our beliefs and our victories. Defeatism, an attitude of pessimism and openness to failure can creep into our heads from time to time. We may think to ourselves: *I'm not good enough, strong enough, smart enough, I'm not worthy*. These thoughts are destructive to our psyche and can tear down our motivation in the blink of an eye. It might happen when we start comparing ourselves with others or when we're faced with repetitive episodes of rejection and failure.

It's imperative to remain positive and shut negative self-talk out of our heads. Countering this automatic urge, like most everything else, starts with awareness. Become highly aware of your patterns and notice the self-critic when it appears. Observe what is happening within you and make a conscious decision to replace the negative talk with a positive one. Convert the annoying, discouraging critic into your very own, personal coach. Identify and acknowledge the greatness within you. Re-energize yourself with your deeper motives. Accept the knowledge that most everyone has this voice within them, a demon we all have to face and eliminate from our minds. Remember that confidence is nothing more than the sum of practice and focus, that mastery is the outcome of overcoming the many challenges and obstacles that present themselves along the way.

CONDITION #9: YOU MUST TAKE ACTION

You can't win the game if you're sitting on the bleachers. We tend to spend our time dreaming and planning, yet without taking one tiny step forward, it's not an objective. It's merely a dream, an idea, a wish, a thought. A reluctance to take action is what separates the doers from the dreamers. You must walk up to the ladder, lift your foot and take that first step. The decision whether you do or not is the most critical factor in the process. No action means no movement, no progress towards your goal.

These very pages you're reading right now started with an idea drowning in fear and excuses. For months, I couldn't get myself to write it. So I took baby steps and started jotting down some notes. Every client, every conversation, every glimpse of enlightenment while walking through the forest, every a-ha moment sitting at a traffic light went into my notebook. Hundreds of pages filled with thoughts, reflections and theories. Far from being a book, it was a collage of everything running through my mind. I wrote until there was nothing left to write. Then, I went around telling everyone I was writing a book when in reality, I was in limbo. I figured if I told enough people, I'd have to live up to my end of the bargain. Eventually, the day came when I powered up my computer, started a new document and stared at a blank screen...for hours! Then, my fingers inched toward the keyboard and entered a few letters: H-A-P-P-Y. And just like that, the first word was typed. Then, I wrote another. One word following the one before it.

A few short months after that inspirational moment, when I stepped outside of my comfort zone, this book was complete. Another item checked off my bucket list. Another product added to the online bookstore. Another goal accomplished. Whether it's praised or criticized makes absolutely no difference. I can only control myself, the actions I took to put these pages together with all my might. Positive intentions, unshakeable work ethic, focus, commitment and tons of coffee. I sincerely hope you enjoyed the read.

Often, people see their goals as an endless ladder rising into the clouds. The thought of reaching their dreams is so demoralizing that they may never take action. To that, I say, commit to taking the first step. Once accomplished, take the next one and repeat the process. Before you know it, you'll be looking down in disbelief at the progress you've made. Reaching your goal will not have been the result of a giant leap but of the commitment to many baby steps which all starts with the very first one.

It's your turn. What dreams and wishes are lingering in that head of yours? What fears and barriers do you need to overcome? Take a deep breath, put your worries aside, break down your goal into a microscopic process and take the first tiny step. Before you know it, you'll be halfway to the finish line looking back in amazement and with a sense of pride. Your success will be a perfect mix of the nine conditions, and it starts with awareness and ownership. It's expanded by knowing what you want and why you want it. It comes into your grasp when you focus on what you control, your willingness to pay the price and your commitment to the process. And finally, it becomes a reality when you genuinely believe in yourself and take the leap of faith.

HAPPINESS IS YOUR RESPONSIBILITY

In the ideal world, we'd all have inspirational leaders paving the way for us, and in turn, we'd all follow suit for those we lead. Each of us interconnected to one another, tapping into each other's Powers, Passions, and Values, creating one massive community of highly engaged and purposeful people. While there is always hope for such a utopia, the road to satisfaction starts within, not without. And while some of the key drivers and motivators in our personal and professional lives may be outside of our control, true empowerment comes from maximizing what is within our grasp and relinquishing whatever isn't.

It starts with the awareness that you always have a choice. That every decision and action you've ever taken and will take is subject to an internal comparison and projection of relative joy. That the moment you connect the dots between a given choice and a heightened level of happiness, you'll pull the trigger and take action. It starts with claiming the following five words as your own:

> My happiness is my responsibility.

Until you take complete responsibility for your happiness, you'll be exposing yourself to negativity, complaining and blaming others. Embrace the truth that, barring genetic disorders and freak accidents, your current reality is the direct result of the sum of the choices you've made and the actions you've taken. Expecting others to contribute to our joy, while convenient, is useless and will only set us up for disappointment. Your happiness is your responsibility, nobody else's. It is imperative that you claim ownership over it. Maintain your Sweet Spot in focus and in balance while continually setting personal objectives and action plans towards the fulfillment of your never-ending need for growth, development and the pursuit of happiness.

Whether at work or in life, whether we have a title or not, the potential for leadership resides in all of us. We each have the power to create and inspire positive change in the world. We each have the ability to reach our highest potentials by gaining awareness and taking bold action. The only question left to ask is "are you ready to become the authentic and inspirational leader you were meant to be?" The choice, as always, is yours.